DHEA...The Fountain of Youth Discovered?

DHEA

The Fountain of Youth Discovered?

Exploring the Link Between Youth and Aging

By Alana Pascal

$12.95 in the U.S.

DHEA...The Fountain of Youth Discovered?
Exploring the Link Between Youth and Aging
By Alana Pascal

Published by:
The Van der Kar Press
P.O. Box 189
Malibu, CA 90265-0189
310-457-6966 / FAX: 310-457-2996

Library of Congress Catalog Card Number 96-60057

ISBN-9645352-1-1

Printed in the United States of America
All Rights Reserved Including Foreign Rights

First Edition 1996

This book may be purchased from the publisher. Please add $3.00 for postage and handling. For more than one book, add an additional $1.50 per book for shipping to the same address.

CREDITS:
Cover Illustration——Valerie Titus
Editor——Anina Maurier with Sheila Alcantara
Graphic Design——Jason D. McKean
Printed by Ben-Wal Printing, Pomona, CA

ACKNOWLEDGMENTS

I would like to express my deep appreciation for those who aided me in the myriad of ways friends do. Thank you to David Diehl, M.D., for his generosity of spirit, particularly for helping me answer some of the more perplexing questions I mused over and for providing me with some very important research materials. I am immensely grateful for the patience and great editorial skills of Anina Maurier and thanks also to Valerie Titus for the wonderful artwork on the cover. A special thank you to Lynne Van der Kar whose generosity, vision and faith in me has made all this possible. To my dear friend, Deborah Van Lelyveld, thank you for inspiring and accommodating a much-needed change in the quality of my life and, finally, thanks to Jackie Aase for getting me out of the house to take long walks that put color back in my cheeks.

Nemaste

CONTENTS

PREFACE

COMPLEMENTARY MEDICINE

The overriding focus of my career in the alternative medicine field is the vision of integrating all the various disciplines into a new form of medicine to meet the challenges of the 21st century. This vision is shared by a number of physician/healers here in the United States. The term "complementary medicine" has been coined for the concept.

This vision of complementary medicine is to bring together various technologies and philosophies to create something greater than the sum of its parts. The mainstream medical community has often been depicted as the unyielding arrogant offender against integration with other methods of healing, but I have witnessed just as much narrow-mindedness in alternative health care workers. Too often both sides come to the table with blinders on, not willing to open their minds to consider other promising approaches. Western medical technology is impressive by any standard. Unfortunately, we have trained many excellent technicians but few healers.

Healers understand that the thoughts and emotions of the patient are as sure an ally or foe as any antibiotic or bacteria.

The chapter on the traditional Chinese system of medical thought is included to introduce and summarize its concepts and theories as they pertain to our discussion of DHEA. The system's philosophy demonstrates a remarkable understanding of the human body valuable to Western medicine and verifiable by Western standards. A combination of the 4,000-year-old Chinese system and the modern Western technological approach could have awe-inspiring results. Harmonious synthesis of the two does require, perhaps, that we not get bogged down in semantics. A synergistic synthesis should facilitate resyntheses with other valid systems of healing.

The medical horizon in this country is broad and very bright indeed. You can personally shape the future of medicine by expecting physicians to be complementary physicians, either trained in reputable alternative modalities or willing to respectfully collaborate with someone who is. We must not let ourselves become victims of the AMA or the FDA. One of the advantages of living in this country is that, as consumers, we wield the ultimate weapon—freedom of choice. I implore you to use it.

FOREWORD

STRESS AND SOCIETY

When I first attempted college, my major was anthropology. I found it intriguing that the mark of a civilized culture was measured by the degree to which it tried to escape the forces and deny the influences of nature. I found it telling that all nature-based cultures were referred to as "primitive," insinuating foolishness and lack of sophistication while advanced cultures were nature-dominating cultures, inferring superiority and maturity. The problem I saw was that for all the supposed intelligence and advancement these cultures possessed, they were the most destructive to themselves and their environments. How intelligent is a society who overpopulates and strips the surrounding ecology, instigating intraspecies conflict, famine and calamity? If we were to witness this behavior in any other creature in nature, it would seem remarkably inane. Within the animal kingdom, civilized man is remarkably dense when it comes to survival.

Most people acknowledge that our modern society is in

crisis. The amount of stress that we face on a day-to-day basis is unprecedented in human history. We are led to believe that our high-consumption lifestyles and the consequential debts we incur are necessary evils to the pursuit of our happiness. This is undoubtedly true in terms of our material acquisitions, but any social scientist, religious leader or observant physician will tell you the price we are paying emotionally, spiritually or physically is too great. The viability of our species is rapidly diminishing not only through the potential of societal and environmental collapse but through the internal breakdown of our bodies. Healthy human beings are the new anomaly. The stress we have decided to cope with and incorporate into our lives is the most insidious enemy to our health.

While investigating the potential of DHEA, I was forced to grapple with the real issue. DHEA should not be considered another potential panacea to a complex problem. Allowing stress to go unchecked in one's life is to ignore the fact of its consequence in mortality. Reducing stress should be a comprehensive process involving lifestyle management, not simply popping a pill to alleviate the symptoms caused by the stress. I take exception to claims that modern man is healthier than ever before. We may have extended our lives with the eradication of what were common infectious diseases through sanitation, antibiotics and vaccines, but a delay in mortality does not sweeten chronic or insidious debilitation. Nor is an assurance against starvation any excuse for obesity——74% of our nation's population over the age of 25 are reported to be overweight. The overall quality of health in the general population is declining. A truly healthy person of any age is a rare thing.

Putting on the skids, simplifying our lives, making them more manageable and reconnecting with community and family are all necessary components to continued health. More than ever, health is not an inalienable right but a privilege. Learning to be healthy, happy and well-loved requires study. Many spend 12-20 years studying to improve their skills to secure a job to earn a living to provide for their material well-being. It makes equally good sense to spend time learning how to be emotionally, spiritually and physically healthy human beings.

DHEA

DHEA is being touted as the fabled "fountain of youth." It is a hormone that is a product of the body's endocrine system which seems to be a key in the healthful resilience of youth. The natural decline over time in the body's production of this hormone is considered fundamental to the aging process. Since clinical evidence does support a link between DHEA and youthfulness, the idea of supplementing it in an aging body is, theoretically, a tempting one. Many of the properties, effects and functions of DHEA are still unknown. Let's examine what research has discovered about this amazingly complex hormone.

Thousands of articles have been written concerning this substance since its discovery in 1934 by Japanese researchers, however it is the flurry of recent research with such dramatic results that is just now beginning to draw popular attention to it. These new studies appear to indicate that DHEA has a positive, symptom-relieving, life-enhancing effect against such broad categories of debilitating and degenerating conditions as:

- insomnia
- depression
- obesity
- high cholesterol and cardiovascular disease
- diabetes
- cancer
- bone density problems [associated with osteoporosis]
- Alzheimer's disease
- viral and bacterial infections
- immunosuppression diseases [e.g. Acquired Immune Deficiency Syndrome (AIDS), Systemic Lupus Erythematosus (SLE) and Chronic Fatigue Immune Deficiency Syndrome (CFIDS)].

A recently reported pilot study done on the effects of DHEA supplementation was conducted on a small sample of participants at the University of California at San Diego. All of the group who had been supplemented with DHEA experienced what they felt subjectively were vast improvements in their ability to cope with stress and a certain *joie de vivre* or sense of well-being. Apparently once this 18-month study was concluded, these improvements had been enough to warrant several of the participants to ask how they might continue taking DHEA themselves.

What is this substance which appears to have such wide-ranging effects?

DHEA, an acronym for *dehydroepiandrosterone*, is the most abundant steroid hormone produced by the adrenal glands of the body. A hormone that has cholesterol as its foundation molecule is called a steroid. DHEA acts as a precursor or pre-hormone (a hormone that breaks down into other hormones) to certain steroid hormones including estrogens and testosterone. As a mineralocorticoid, it helps regulate the biocritical electrolytes, sodium and potassium.

DHEA's role is unique. Recent research has revealed that its function is greater than its previous designation as solely a precursor hormone might suggest. Intriguing information now shows that there are specific receptor sites on cells explicitly for DHEA. This fact points to a much broader function of the hormone, but its intricacies are still a mystery. It has been found that DHEA acts as an inhibitory hormone blocking the negative effects of other corticoids which are overproduced by a body in stress. In short, this means that DHEA appears to counteract some of the impact of stress. This could be a critical link to DHEA's ameliorating effects on many degenerative conditions associated with aging. No one at this time can state whether the effects of DHEA come from the hormone itself or from the sex hormones and other steroids into which it is converted. Little is truly understood about the hormone's obviously complex functions within the human body.

What is definitely known about DHEA:

— Only primates and humans produce it.

— It is the most abundant steroid in human plasma.

— It is metabolized in the adrenal cortex and is found most abundantly in the brain and the skin.

— Heredity is a factor in the ranges of an individual's DHEA production.

— DHEA is the major adrenal androgen precursor falling in the category of what are referred to as 17-ketosteroids whose principal action include androgenic and anabolic functions. [An androgen, as it is produced by the cortex of the adrenal glands, is a weakened version (five times less potent) of the testosterone produced by male gonads. Although associated with masculinizing effects, its secretion occurs in both sexes. This adrenal-produced male sex hormone is an essential component of libido (sex drive) in females. Anabolic function is the activity of generation and regeneration in reference to the building of muscle mass or the promotion of metabolic activity.]

— The range of naturally occurring levels of DHEA is so wide that average levels produced in one person can be vastly lower or higher than normal levels in otherwise similar individuals.

— When the DHEA hormone is metabolized, it produces a metabolite called DHEAS *(dehydroepiandrosterone sulfate)*. The amount of DHEAS found in the bloodstream is the most reliable marker to determine how well a body is utilizing DHEA.

— A fetus begins manufacturing DHEA in the second trimester which stimulates the placenta to produce estrogen and progesterone, thereby allowing the pregnancy to progress.

— At birth, production of DHEA stops to slowly resume again at age 7-8 in preparation for puberty. DHEA levels continue to rise until about the age of 25-28 after which it steadily declines around the age of 70 to 10-15% of the peak levels.

— Man's average adrenal production of DHEA, approximately 30 mg. per day, is roughly twice the amount of a woman's production. DHEA has been found to be synthesized in the skin and women naturally produce less of it. These facts may account for why a man's skin generally tends to wrinkle and age less quickly than a woman's.

— DHEA appears to function as a neurosteroid. The highest concentrations of DHEAS are found in the brain.

Steroid Biosynthesis Pathways

— Based on the most recent studies, many researchers feel that DHEA and DHEAS levels are the most meaningful indicators of biological aging that the endocrine system presents.

— Most importantly, DHEA has a specific function at a cellular level which is still shrouded in mystery.

Compelling to researchers is evidence that low DHEA/ DHEAS levels appear to be associated with the onset of a number of medical conditions, including rheumatoid arthritis, heart disease and some of the more bewildering syndromes related to immunosuppression. Apparently, lowered DHEA/

DHEAS levels can also provide a diagnostic index to the development and progression of diseases like cancer, HIV and AIDS.

Is it possible that taking this substance could return us to the health and vigor of our younger adult years?

It must be emphasized here that replacing a hormone that the body itself naturally reduces in quantity at a certain age is no casual undertaking. For better or for worse, post-menopausal women have had the availability of hormone replacement therapy (HRT) for the past three decades. Studies conducted over those years have revealed HRT to be a complicated matter. Although HRT was "hyped" as being the greatest boon to the menopausal population, subsequent study results have proved less enthusiastic. Still, we know a great deal about HRT and its potential side effects. However, HRT still requires serious consideration and we know a lot more about it than we do about DHEA.

The glowing reports that have been published recently about DHEA raise many questions. At what age, at what dosage and for how long does a patient take DHEA? How much is an individual at risk if the DHEA treatment is mismanaged? Could it also result in a physiological dependency? What are the potential long-term effects? These and other important questions need to be answered. Only with substantial investments of time and money in research can these concerns be properly addressed and accurately determined.

Nonetheless, information available from the most recent studies is exciting. Let's take a look at the current research and consider the implications of the clinical evidence already compiled.

THE BEGINNINGS — DHEA PRESENTED

In 1979, evidence of the remarkable potential of DHEA was presented at the Gordon Conference on Aging in Santa Barbara, California. Arthur Schwartz, M.D., stunned the assembled scientists and researchers when he presented 10 years of research relating to this mysterious adrenal steroid.

In the early 1970's, Dr. Schwartz, as a researcher studying life span and metabolic activation of carcinogens, became intrigued by an idea. He believed that steroids, because of their chemical similarity to certain carcinogens, could compete for receptors on a cell's surface. He reasoned that if he could find the right steroid to block these receptors, he would be able to inhibit the development of cancerous cells. Findings of the Imperial Cancer Research Fund, a long-term British study of the residents on the island of Guernsey, begun in 1961 and headed up by R.D. Bulbrook, M.D., revealed that there appeared to be a link in low DHEAS levels and the occurrence of breast cancer among the 5,000 women in the study. Dr. Schwartz was excited by these findings. He speculated that administration of the DHEA steroid might protect the tissues from cancer.

Dr. Schwartz used powerful carcinogens (including aflatoxin, a fungus commonly found in corn, peanuts and milk products) on cell cultures. Schwartz was excited to discover that when DHEA was added to the cultures, the high rate of cell death, mutation and transformation the researcher had expected did not occur. In an effort to prove his hypothesis concerning steroid receptor replacement, he tried DHEA analogues.

Analogues are substances that are structurally similar to another substance with only slight differences between them. He tried different DHEA analogues with the original steroid molecules still intact. None of the analogues worked with the same stunning success as the original base compound of DHEA. He realized then that it was not the steroid portion of the DHEA molecule that provided the protective effect but apparently something else within DHEA itself. He had the benefit of several studies that had been conducted in which DHEA was shown to be a potent inhibitor of the enzyme G6PD (glucose 6, phosphate dihydrogenase). He began to piece the puzzle together. It was this assembled puzzle that he presented to his colleagues at the Gordon Conference on Aging.

The enzyme G6PD is the first step in both of the two different ways in which the body uses glucose. As a rule, glucose is broken down in an *energy-yielding pathway*. This pathway provides energy for the body's needs. But there is another route for glucose, the *biosynthetic pathway*, in which G6PD will initiate turning glucose into fatty acids for future use, as well as into the nucleic acids RNA and DNA. In this biosynthetic pathway, G6PD is responsible for the creation of fat and new cells. If DHEA inhibited G6PD in this biosynthetic pathway, then perhaps it also blocked the cancer-causing mutation potential of a cell.

Cancer develops when changes in a cell's metabolism causes an abnormal growth pattern. G6PD appears to cause these cell abnormalities. It appears that DHEA blocks that substance's action within the biosynthetic pathway.

In addition, Dr. Schwartz added to his theory the results of the work of Dr. Terence Yen who was at that time a biochemist at Eli Lilly, a major pharmaceutical company. Dr. Yen had made an intriguing discovery. DHEA's ability to block the G6PD pathway and thereby inhibit fatty acid production also caused laboratory mice who were genetically programmed to become obese to remain slim and sleek and to live longer. This anti-obesity capability apparently came from DHEA pushing more of the glucose toward the energy-yielding pathway and away from the biosynthetic, fat-producing pathway.

For more than 50 years, scientists have known that certain dietary restrictions which counteract obesity do reduce the incidence of cancer, delay the onset of age-related diseases, such as arteriosclerosis and arthritis, and extend life span. Unfortunately, achieving these life-saving benefits requires a lifetime of discipline. Being able to eat freely while reaping anti-obesity benefits would be fantastic. Yen's experiments demonstrated that, despite eating their average caloric amounts, the lab animals efficiently burned off the calories and consequently remained slim. DHEA could counteract the effects of cancer-conducive conditions like obesity and help prevent runaway growth of cancer cells, a double blow against the development of cancer.

Dr. Schwartz conducted in-depth studies to attempt to discover DHEA's "active ingredients." In these subsequent studies, neither DHEA nor DHEAS was found to deactivate G6PD. Instead, a sulfatide version that represents one percent of the free DHEA was declared active against G6PD. Unfortunately, DHEA sulfatide is highly unstable, breaking down rapidly into DHEAS by the time it enters the bloodstream.

The presentation by Dr. Schwartz in 1979 surprised the audience and piqued the interest of scientists, particularly one, Dr. William Regelson, M.D. Dr. Regelson has gone on to become perhaps the foremost advocate of the wonders of DHEA and is well known for his studies on melatonin. Since 1979, Dr. Regelson has spent years studying aging and longevity and has helped fund research on an eclectic list of potential modalities. In 1990, Dr. Regelson and colleagues Dr. Mohammed Kalimi and Dr. Roger Loria, published a book now considered the bible of DHEA research, *The Biological Role of Dehydroepiandrosterone (DHEA)*.

It was Dr. Regelson, along with Senator Alan Cranston from California and Don Yarborough, a former gubernatorial candidate from Texas, who set up the Fund for Integrative Biomedical Research (FIBER) in the late 1970's. This organization was established to research promising anti-aging therapies with the hope of keeping potential therapies from being buried in the lengthy peer-reviewal process.

It was FIBER, under the direction of Dr. Regelson that funded Schwartz for further studies on DHEA into the 1980's. DHEA became one of Dr. Regelson's pet projects. In all of the studies that he and his colleagues supported through their funding, Dr. Regelson's primary objective was to find a "biomarker of aging." He believed that for intervention in aging to be successful, there must be physical signposts or measurable biomarkers that allow a researcher or clinician to know how well a particular regimen is working. After FIBER closed it doors, Dr. Regelson continued to conduct DHEA research. Searching for endocrine markers for biological aging has become a significant focus of anti-aging research.

Let's review briefly the endocrine system before looking at how long-term unrelenting stress affects it.

THE ENDOCRINE SYSTEM

    The endocrine system is made up of a number of glandular tissues and organs that secrete "chemical messengers" directly into the bloodstream. These chemical messengers are hormones that regulate and integrate bodily functions between cells and organ systems. Researchers concede that, for the most part, the endocrine system is a great mysterious web of actions and interactions whose functions are fundamental to immunity, digestion and assimilation, reproduction, maturation and aging. It integrates perceptions to produce physical reactions, determines metabolism and bone integrity and manages the bioelectrical systems of the body by maintaining the electrolytes—sodium, potassium, calcium and magnesium. The endocrine system is so integral that it is *the* foundation of health. All bodily systems are subject to its output, input and management. Consequently, the endocrine system should not be ignored in any disease or condition, nor should it be manipulated recklessly.

The endocrine system is made up of 12 known structures (and a number of tissue sites). It is speculated that further investigation will reveal a number more. Listed (as they occur from the top of the head down the body) are its known structures:

- pineal
- hypothalamus
- pituitary
- thyroid
- parathyroid glands
- thymus
- pancreas
- the gastrointestinal mucosa
- adrenals
- kidneys
- testes
- ovaries

The endocrine system is an integrated system. This integration is accomplished by the nervous system which produces electroneurological messages and stimulates hormonal signals transmitted throughout the body to cells. The nervous system can transmit its messages very rapidly through endocrine products called neurotransmitters. Certain neurotransmitters, like adrenaline, noradrenaline and dopamine work over a short distance (such as on adjacent cells). For the most part, it is the central part of the adrenal gland, the medulla, that is the source of these chemicals. Stimulated by a special ganglion (a very sophisticated nerve structure), these substances are eventually released into the bloodstream just like other hormones. It is the production of adrenaline that provides the adrenal rush with which we are all familiar.

The body is controlled basically by two nervous systems, the central nervous system (CNS) and the peripheral nervous system (PNS). Within the PNS, there are two divisions: the *somatic* system that moves skeletal muscles and relays messages to the central nervous system and the *autonomic* nervous system, principally concerned with circulation, the internal organs and sexual function. The endocrine system, part of the autonomic nervous system, relies on a slower hormonal transmission of its signals through the bloodstream in order to sustain long-term effects.

These specific endocrine glands and their respective functions are featured in relation to DHEA:

• <u>Hypothalamus</u> controls most neurological functions and is influenced by higher systems of the forebrain. The hypothalamus has the capability of translating neurological impulses and stimuli into hormonal signals. These electro-neurological signals are translated by the hypothalamus into release factors. It produces these release factors to stimulate the anterior pituitary to produce its own hormones that stimulate hormone production generally. These release factors include:

— corticotropin releasing factor (CRF) responsible for the production of ACTH from the pituitary,

— growth hormone releasing factor (GRF) responsible for the release of growth hormone,

— thyrotropin releasing factor (TRF) responsible for stimulating of TSH (thyroid-stimulating hormone) and

— gonadotropin releasing factor (GnRF) responsible for

stimulating the gonads to produce reproductive hormones.

• <u>Anterior pituitary</u> takes the messages of the release factors and produces stimulating hormones that signal the glands to produce their hormones. The list includes:

— ACTH (adrenocorticotropin) which stimulates the adrenal cortex hormones

— TSH (thyroid stimulating hormone) which stimulates the thyroid gland

— GH (Growth hormone or somatropin) which stimulates bone and muscle growth during the childhood years of development.

[Although GH production in adults is almost identical to that in children, GH in the adult exerts an anti-insulin effect increasing blood sugar levels and inhibiting the body's ability to utilize glucose. This leads to the breakdown of fat for fatty acids to be sent into the energy cycle. This type of GH function is dependent on the adrenal cortex production of cortisol, so that in times of stress, the muscles and heart will use available fatty acids rather than glucose for fuel. This reserves glucose exclusively for the brain's use, it being the only source of fuel for the brain. This function of GH is important when we consider stress and endocrine relationships as they relate to disease, most notably to immune system impairment.]

— and various reproductive hormones.

[In women, follicle-stimulating hormone (FSH), responsible for stimulating the ripening of an egg from the ovary, luteinizing hormone (LH), responsible for the production of estrogen and progesterone. In men, the comparable hormone to LH is the interstitial cell-stimulating hormone (ICSH) which stimulates the production of testosterone. FSH in men (sometimes referred to as germinal-stimulating hormone) stimulates testicular cells to produce sperm.]

• Thyroid gland forms thyroxin (T4) and triiodothyronine (T3). The levels of secretion of these hormones determine one's metabolism. These hormones are made of iodine and tyrosine, an amino acid. The thyroid is also responsible for calcitonin which is important in bone and calcium metabolism. Calcitonin inhibits the body from taking too much calcium from the bones.

• Parathyroid glands are four "b b"-size glands imbedded within the "wings" of the butterfly-like structure of the thyroid —two on each side. These glands are responsible for the production of parathyroid hormone which acts to raise blood levels of calcium. This hormone acts on the bones and the kidneys in order to maintain appropriate levels of calcium in the blood for ensuring that the bio-electrical systems, particularly of the heart, nerves and cellular membranes, have adequate calcium to keep them functioning properly. The parathyroids are integral to the maintenance of good bone integrity.

• Thymus gland is the "graduate school" for immune factors transforming white blood cells into specialized defense units. These defense units include T-killer, T-helper and T-suppressor cells as well as the cytokines called interleukins.

• Pancreas contains two types of cells alpha and beta. Alpha cells produce digestive enzymes for the duodenum/small intestine phase of digestion. Beta cells produce insulin in the islets of Langerhans. Insulin is responsible for moving sugar from the bloodstream into cells to produce energy. Maintaining proper blood sugar levels is critical to health.

• Adrenal gland has two parts:

1. the adrenal medulla is the central portion of the gland producing the catecholamines epinephrine (also called adrenaline), norepinephrine (also called noradrenaline) and dopamine which act as neurotransmitters. Catecholamines, derived from tyrosine, are based on the amino acid phenylalanine which, passing through a series of enzymatic reactions, goes on to produce the catecholamines. This is the order of their production: Phenylalanine—p-tyrosine—Dopa—Dopamine—Norepinephrine—Epinephrine. Dopamine is crucial to fine motor control and immune function, as well as motivation. Like DHEA, there is an age-related dramatic decline in dopamine-containing neurons of the brain after the age of 45. Its decline is reputed to be one of the sources of the gradual age-related decrease in sex drive of both males and females. It is an *abnormal* decline in dopamine that is associated with Parkinson's disease. Dopamine goes on to form norepinephrine. After conversion, norepinephrine represents nearly 20% of the adrenal medullar output while epinephrine, the next neuro-transmitter produced, results in the remaining 80%. For the medulla to produce epinephrine, it requires an enzyme (phenethanolamine-N-methyl transferase) that is dependent on high concentrations of glucocorticoids from the adrenal cortex. This fact will become more pertinent as we study the impact stress has on the body and DHEA's role in mediating it. The reactions of norepinephrine and epineph-

rine are generally similar. Both increase the force of the contraction of the heart, break down fats which raise the level of circulating free fatty acids, speed metabolic rate and enhance alertness by their action on the brain. There are, however, two important differences between them. Norepinephrine causes constriction of all blood vessels—except the coronary vessels of the heart. Epinephrine constricts coronary vessels while increasing heart rate, but dilates the bronchioles of the lungs and the vessels in skeletal muscles and the liver. It breaks down glycogen in the liver and tissues, pouring glucose into circulation while norepinephrine does not. This is very important to the stress cycle, because if left unmediated, high epinephrine levels will cause disruptions in other endocrine relationships.

2. the adrenal cortex surrounds the medulla. It is the major site of steroid production of cortisol, corticosterone, aldosterone, and the "mother" hormone of the steroids, DHEA, which in turn breaks down into the androgens, estrogens and progesterone.

• Testes are responsible for the production of the steroid hormone testosterone. Testosterone is the masculinizing hormone primarily produced in male gonads. In women, it is usually referred to as an androgen and is primarily produced from the cortex of the adrenals. Androgen production of testosterone is responsible for stimulating hair growth under the arm and pubic region. A lack of this androgen creates thin hair coverage in those areas and could be an indication of DHEA deficiency.

• Ovaries are responsible for the production of the steroid hormone estrogen. There are three forms of estrogen: esterone, estriol and estradiol, estradiol being the most important. Estrogen causes the blood vessels to become more elastic, providing a protective role over a woman's vasculature during pregnancy in order for her to withstand the associated changes in high blood pressure. When menopause occurs, elasticity is lost due to the ovarian shut down of estrogen production. Thereafter a woman's risk of cardiovascular disease becomes the same as it is for a man.

STRESS

Stress is a loaded word. It is fundamental to being alive and is not necessarily something bad; nor is it something to be entirely avoided. To live a full and rewarding life means to encounter and cope with stress. In fact, in order for the body to function properly, it must utilize stress. However, stress becomes a problem when an unrelenting level of stressors (be they physical, environmental, mental or emotional) causes the body to produce an abundance of harmful chemicals.

Ironically, the most stressful moments in my practice as an alternative practitioner have been while collaborating with physicians on a patient suffering from "adrenal burnout." My efforts to explain to the doctors the progression of this condition by describing adrenal excess, then insufficiency and eventual adrenal failure often met with stone silence and a polite clearing of the throat. I knew it was semantics and the scope of the concept rather than the actual clinical condition which caused the confusion and discomfort between my medical colleagues and myself. For a conventionally trained physician, adrenal problems mean Cushing's disease (adrenal excess) or Addison's disease (adrenal insufficiency) or adrenal collapse, three separate and distinct conditions associated with underlying pathologies. What I was describing was a progressive disorder through the three categories. In its early clinical stages, a "blown adrenal" syndrome is comprised of a large and varied bundle of symptoms and conditions like food sensitivities, insomnia, immune deficiencies, debilitating fatigue, depression, premenstrual tension, menopause symptoms, blood sugar regulation problems (including non-insulin dependent diabetes, hypoglycemia, hyperinsulinemia) and hyperactivity now classed under the catch-all phrase Attention Deficit Disorder (ADD). In its later stages, this syndrome culminates in serious degenerative disease. I was associating a mysterious constellation of symptoms with an adrenal syndrome, symptoms which in their various combinations have been baffling the medical community.

Because of the unusually large proportion of women suffering from these "nonspecific" complaints, the politics of dealing with "female complaints" had been ascribing the conditions in women to the "complex emotional/hormonal problems that are inherently female." Many patients were being told by conventional practitioners that perhaps counseling or psychotherapy was needed as the solution.

Over the years, some of the cases were eventually diagnosed as Chronic Fatigue Immune Deficiency Syndrome (CFIDS). It was made a legitimate medical condition by the Center for Disease Control in the late 1980's. More recently, fibromyalgia covered the symptoms that did not include viral markers (EBV, CMV, herpes etc.) that are associated with CFIDS. These labels made "vague complaints" real, but the syndrome continues to have no agreed-upon treatment plan, leaving victims with a diagnosis but no cure. In the meantime, there continues to be a steady increase in the number of patients who suffer from fatigue (sometimes debilitating), depression, immune deficiencies, chronic swollen glands, and blood sugar regulation issues that don't qualify under the CFIDS or fibromyalgia classifications. This constellation of symptoms with no strong laboratory markers (most individuals' blood tests fall within normal ranges) has contributed more to the increasingly common mutiny from conventional medicine than perhaps any other condition.

I knew what it was——**stress**——and the "vague symptoms" were the subclinical manifestations of the breakdown of the endocrine system. My distress as a practitioner has been that I knew what I was dealing with, but the tools that I had to provide a cure took a great deal of time and involved **major** lifestyle changes in patients, and therefore were very difficult to accommodate. As the evidence of DHEA research mounted, it appeared that the mysterious occurrences of these non-specific complaints were finding a common laboratory marker ——low serum DHEAS levels. Most importantly, the research showed that by providing supplemental DHEA, a significant number of these types of vague complaints disappeared. It was of great relief to have a pill to recommend to patients. For the vast majority of Americans, pills are much easier to take than the efforts involved in making serious lifestyle modifications. Do not get me wrong; serious assessments and removal of stress and stressful living habits are mandatory to re-establishing balance and health, regardless of the ingestion of any medication including DHEA. **These steps cannot be ignored.**

One of the most telling symptoms of adrenal "blow out" is abnormal sleep patterns. The pineal gland is responsible for determining circadian and diurnal cycles. Circadian cycles involve daily and seasonal fluctuations of body functions based on the amount of light exposure. The body functions most influenced are the wake/sleep cycle, the menstrual cycle, growth and eating cycles. The diurnal cycle affects functions associated with daytime activities.

It is known that the adrenals begin their daily production of hormones, including DHEA, between 2:30 and 4:00 a.m. which will stimulate a gentle waking cycle. When the adrenals are stressed, many individuals will wake up not gently, but startled awake suddenly during those hours, sometimes in a sweat, heart pounding, agitated and unable to fall back to sleep. They will toss and turn until adrenal production falls off again, generally between the hours of 4-5 a.m. Unfortunately, if they fall back to sleep, their natural sleep pattern is disturbed and waking later can be difficult. Many individuals struggle through the first few hours after rising, shuffling through their daily routines feeling exhausted and foggy during the morning to midday hours until the system is overridden again.

When I was a child spending the summers on the dairy farms and cattle ranches of my family, the normal waking schedule of the farmers and ranchers was to be up and out working by 4:30 a.m. Both grandmothers began cooking at that hour to have breakfast ready for the men at first light. In convents, monasteries, ashrams and temples throughout the world, morning prayers are begun at or near these hours. This is our natural rhythm. Until three generations ago, most Americans lived rural lives that were more in line with this natural order. For many of us now, our modern work schedules have been altered to "banking hours"——with arrival at the work place around 9-10 a.m. This is a subtle example of how modern man, within the past two generations, has denied natural rhythms in ways that not so subtly affect his health and well-being. Those of you who have had the experience of living without clocks probably have noticed there is a rhythm that begins to permeate one's activities. It is common to rise at first light and fall asleep when natural daylight ends based on the season, not the clock, sleeping, or more aptly put, hibernating, more in the long winter hours. This is the natural circadian cycle. With the current popularity of melatonin, based on the premise of the pineal melatonin-serotonin-sleep clock connection, one can see how artificial replacement of these chemicals is just one more attempt to ignore the importance of slowing down and becoming a more *natural* human being.

STRESS IN THEORY

I do not pretend to have discovered the "blown adrenal" syndrome. That honor goes to Hans Selye, M.D., a Canadian physician who creatively turned his ineptness at lab work into an insightful theory on the maladaptive phases of stress in the human body, the theory of the General Adaptation Syndrome (GAS). It is time for conventional medical practitioners to dust off Dr. Selye's research and take a hard look at his theory. It may provide a key to understanding the bewildering health problems emerging in the 1990's.

Dr. Hans Selye was 19 when he entered medical school in Austria after the First World War. Dr. Selye believes it was the guileless curiosity of his youth that started him on his life's work, after noticing a common "syndrome of just being sick." These symptoms were generally ignored by the doctors under whom he was studying. He questioned why his superiors did not address this general condition. He was told that a diagnosis was based on the differentiating characteristics to this general "syndrome of just being sick," e.g. rash, specific swollen glands, variances in blood chemistries etc. Nonspecific complaints that included diffuse pain, fatigue, appetite and weight loss were not a disease in and of itself. His continued inquiries into the syndrome were met with considerably less than encouragement from his colleagues. No one understood what relevance these complaints had in disease causation.

Despite this lack of support, Dr. Selye persisted and 10 years later, as a lab technician studying sex hormones in Montreal, he noticed that when he injected impure extracts of sex compounds into his lab mice, a persistent group of changes occurred in the animals. His observations included the swelling of the adrenal cortex, shrinking of the thymus, gastrointestinal ulcers, weight loss, inability of the body to appropriately regulate body temperature, the disappearance of eosinophils (a specific type of white blood cell specific to immune function), alteration of body chemicals affecting body fluids and tissues and, most importantly in Dr. Selye mind, changes in the body's response to what should have remained only localized inflammatory conditions. The whole body of the mice had rallied against assault and produced some kind of general anti-inflammatory hormone throughout the body, rather than limiting inflammation to a localized area as expected.

Was this anti-inflammatory hormone being produced by the swollen adrenals? This research became Dr. Selye's consuming passion and,despite having received many honors for his work, his theory has never been entirely embraced by the medical community as an approach to understanding the subtleties of endocrine relationships and their link to degenerative disease.

THE *GENERAL ADAPTATION SYNDROME*

Without parallel, the body is one of the most adaptable machines ever created and its ability to withstand abuse is nothing short of magical. Dr. Selye formed a theory concerning unrelenting stress and the changes the body undergoes to deal with it. He called this physiological alchemy the *General Adaptation Syndrome.*

According to him, the General Adaptation Syndrome (GAS) has three phases, the *alarm phase*, the *resistant* or *maladaptive phase* and the *exhaustion phase*. The whole series of physiological events which the GAS incorporates are first stimulated and later sustained by the adrenal glands. Dr. Selye's work is most noted for the insight his research provided in identifying and articulating the function of the hormone products of these two glandular attachments to the kidneys, the adrenal glands.

THE ADRENALS

These two small endocrine glands singly sit atop both respective kidneys, hence the name "adrenal" (from Latin, of course, "renal" is an adjective for kidneys, "ad-" is a prefix for "near" or "at"). Interestingly, the right adrenal is pyramid-shaped while the left is crescent-shaped. The normal adrenal gland weighs between 5 and 7 grams. A male adrenal is on average about 30% heavier than a female's. The inner core of an adrenal gland is called the medulla. It is the medulla that produces the hormones adrenaline, noradrenaline and dopamine.

Adrenaline (also called epinephrine) is a hormone most of us recognize. An "adrenaline rush" is an experience most of us have endured at least once in our lives. Sometimes referred to as the "fight or flight" response, this adrenal response is a primal rudimentary reaction of the body's survival instinct. Upon activation, these glands increase their output of adrenaline and noradrenaline nearly tenfold, with adrenaline accounting for 80% of the output.

THE FIRST MAGIC ACT

When a stressor is recognized as serious but manageable—for example a police officer facing an armed criminal—his training elicits more noradrenaline to be secreted. The noradrenaline directs sugar to the brain to enhance mental acuity (rather than delivering sugar to the muscles), thereby slowing down the adrenaline rush to enable him to manage his primal instinct to take aim or take cover. It is important to understand that what one may perceive as frightening, another person may manage calmly. This perception is affected as much by societal and cultural experience as by specific, individualized training. Researchers will tell you that a belief system is literally incorporated within the hypothalamus which can interpret the forebrain's messages through other structures (namely the hippocampus, the thalamus and amygdala) to elicit bodily responses in terms of those beliefs. This is an amazing process and tells us something about the potential of cultivating the power of the mind.

The adrenal cortex is the outer portion of the adrenal gland. Its function is primarily affected by adrenocorticotropin (ACTH), a pituitary hormone specific to the adrenal cortex. It is the cortex that produces steroid hormones—hormones whose foundation molecules are cholesterol. The cortex has three zones:

- *Zona glomerulosa* (outer layer) produces mostly mineralocorticoids and is not ACTH-dependent as are the other two zones.
- *Zona fasciculata* (middle layer)
- *Zona reticularis* (next to the medulla).

The fasciculata and the reticulates produce steroid hormones. Steroid hormones are glucocorticoids, 17-ketosteroid androgens and estrogens. All these hormones are dependent upon ACTH for secretion. DHEA appears to be produced in all three zones. DHEA is classified as a mineralocorticoid as well as falling under the 17-ketosteroid group.

WHAT IS STRESS?

If we come to understand stress as the "state manifested by a specific syndrome which consists of all the nonspecifically induced changes within a body"—nonspecific disease complaints —we will realize that stress has its own characteristic form and composition *but no particular cause*. This kind of a statement requires a great leap of faith in a scientific mind. It bypasses a few synapses much the same way quantum physics rattles a

Newtonian physicist. Stress is a synergy of endocrinological impairments that creates a syndrome about which conventional medicine has established a policy of differential diagnosis. These symptoms are more appropriately termed a "state." This state is the root of degenerative disease conditions.

COPING WITH STRESS

The ability of an individual to offset acute infectious conditions, as well as chronic degenerative diseases, is related to the individual's inherent reserve of adaptive energy. You may think of adaptive energy as the "trust fund" of your body contributed to by your genetic ancestors. Each individual inherits a certain amount of adaptive energy, the amount of which is determined by his genetic profile and background. This is what may be called one's constitution. Depending on each individual's circumstances, this reserve of adaptive energy is limited to a greater or lesser degree and should be guarded—not spent foolishly. Adaptive energy is used in the body's processes of coping with stressors. An individual can deplete this biological trust fund by poor lifestyle practices, such as a bad diet or lack of exercise.

DHEA appears to be fundamental to one's constitution. DHEA levels are at their highest peaks during early youth when cancer, arthritis or cardiovascular disease rarely strikes. The evidence of DHEA research highlights its great ability to alleviate the impact of stress-produced chemicals which otherwise can lead to the onset of many chronic degenerative diseases. As DHEA production declines, the tendency to develop these diseases increases. There are hereditary factors in individual levels of DHEA production as well as sex differences. Also, prenatal stressors in the mother can influence fetal DHEA production and have life-long effects. More about this later.

When confronted with physical or psychological stress, a variety of reactions take place. The hypothalamus is the first member of the endocrine system to acknowledge and process information in analyzing a dangerous or life-threatening situation. Located at the base of the brain above the pituitary gland, it is ideally located to exert control over the endocrine and autonomic nervous systems while being controlled by the higher forebrain centers receiving sensory messages. These messages are "interpreted" by the hypothalamus which then helps generate an individual's perceptions, emotions, and cognition. The hypothalamus is responsible for how you interpret what is perceived. Is the situation manageable or dangerously threatening?

The two extremes in attitude relevant to stress management are popularly characterized as "high strung" or "laid back." In physiological terms, they are expressed as sympathetic dominant (excitable) as opposed to parasympathetic dominant (calmer).

The appreciation of serious danger initiates a sequence of biological events called an adrenergic or sympathetic response, more descriptively the "fight or flight" response. This type of stress response is intended to be of short duration, lasting seconds to a few minutes. It is a remarkable cascade of chemical and electrical processes designed to increase our physical ability to survive immanent danger in our natural world. Unfortunately, many individuals in our modern world are "fighting the tiger" a number of times a day. This pattern of adrenal stress, if not managed or successfully removed, will eventually lead to very dangerous levels of ACTH-stimulated glucocorticoids.

By looking at each phase individually, we can chart the progression of the adrenals' involvement in chronic degenerative diseases, particularly those associated with aging. Think of the endocrine system as a complex spider web of actions, interactions and reactions. Touching one strand distorts and affects many others, causing vibrations throughout the web. Watch what happens when we touch the adrenal cortex strand of the web. The series of events is important. In an healthy individual, DHEA is fundamental to managing the adrenals' impact on the various systems that are interconnected via this web.

THE ALARM PHASE

In the alarm phase, inflictions from stressors cause the adrenals to hyperfunction——swelling them in size and increasing their hormonal output to help cope with the stress. Stress induces a rise in a pituitary-released hormone, adrenocorticotropin (ACTH). ACTH stimulates the adrenal cortex to synthesize and release steroid hormones that act as anti-inflammatory agents. These agents were coined glucocorticoids (GCS) by Dr. Selye and act as the mediators of the chronic response to stress. Glucocorticoids include cortisol, cortisone and corticosterone. GCS were designed by our physiology to be used to combat the potential of pain and injury and are meant only to be circulating in the body for short periods of time——minutes to hours (if no injury occurred) to a few days (with injury). However, if stress is chronic, the brain will override a shut-off signal and continue to stimulate the pituitary to produce ACTH. This continued stimulation of the cortex by the pituitary leads to *hypertrophy* or excess growth and enlargement of the adrenal cortex. This enlargement of the cortex leads to elevated levels of glucocorticoids being produced. These glucocorticoids will eventually begin to circulate freely, initiating a very dangerous cycle of destruction.

THE RESISTANT OR MALADAPTIVE PHASE

The glucocorticoids are potent mobilizers of fuel and amino acids, breaking down protein stores while enhancing fat synthesis. This form of fat synthesis is responsible for visceral fat, the type of fat deposited in pads across the abdomen, hips and thighs commonly referred to as "middle age spread." This sustained mobilization of fuel and amino acids is a catabolic or destructive process, tearing down muscle for these stores of fuel—glucose.

Elevated glucocorticoids have been implicated in cardiovascular disease, blood sugar regulation problems (like insulin resistance and hyperinsulinemia) fat accumulation, compromised immune function, exhaustion and chronic degenerative diseases.

GLUCOCORTICOIDS

Elevated levels of glucocorticoids are the most damaging effects of stress. Glucocorticoids and mineralocorticoids are essentially arbitrary designations in that most glucocorticoids have mineralocorticoid-like characteristics and vice versa. The principal glucocorticoid is cortisol (pharmaceutically called hydrocortisone). Most of us who are already familiar with cortisone therapy for arthritis and other inflammatory conditions are also familiar with the side effects and damage it can cause when taken over long periods of time. The swelling and bloated condition many people acquire from long-term use of this synthetic compound is due to the effects of the mineralocorticoidal aspect of this complex system. Gluco-corticoids regulate catecholamine production of the adrenal medulla while catecholamines stimulate ACTH release from the pituitary. Glucocorticoids are most noted for their mobilization of glucose for fuel and amino acids.

During and immediately after a stressful situation, cortisol enhances the synthesis of a number of proteins, particularly those which increase the production of enzymes critical to fat synthesis. During the recovery from stress, fat synthesis is improved. Dietary intake is more likely to be converted into fat than energy once the danger is over.

This is important when treating obesity. The restriction of calories in an effort to reduce body fat is interpreted by the body as stress. After the desired weight is attained and former food intake levels return, the lost weight is usually regained with extra. This additional weight gain is the result of glucocorticoid stress responses turning the calories into fat as a survival mechanism because of the recent stress it had just experienced from the diet restriction. This is the body's attempt to set aside reserves for future emergencies including future intake restrictions.

Glucocorticoids get their name from the characteristic that these steroid substances raise blood sugar. They do this by acting as an insulin inhibitor decreasing insulin production and blocking the body's ability to take up glucose (sugar) into the cellular tissue. This ability to inhibit insulin can also cause insulin resistance. Insulin resistance is a very serious condition significantly enhancing the risk of cardiovascular disease. Part of aging is increased insulin resistance. In fact, it is considered an endocrine marker for aging. It should be noted that increases in either insulin or in glucocorticoids will cause a decline in DHEA levels.

Hypoglycemia is very stressful to the body and the body will respond by increasing glucocorticoid production. When glucocorticoid levels rise due to long-term stress reactions (as they do in untreated cases of hypoglycemia), very dramatic effects are seen in the immune system. Macrophage activity, T-cell function as well as production of interleukin-2 are all diminished. All three are very necessary immune components most notably lacking in autoimmune diseases like AIDS and SLE.

GROWTH HORMONE

With a rise of ACTH, there is a commensurate rise in the release of growth hormone (GH). This hormone is responsible for the synthesis of new protein needed to fight infection or repair injured tissue. If neither physical injury or infection occurs, growth hormone will stimulate the reuse of amino acids released through the glucocorticoids' catabolic effect. An excessive amount of growth hormone circulating throughout the body has been associated with stimulation of cancer growth.

DHEA's greatest contribution appears to lie in alleviating the impact of stress and the age-induced ravages of these glucocorticoids. This fact alone may warrant the epithet "fountain of youth."

THE ADRENAL EXHAUSTION PHASE

If the level of stress continues, the eventual exhaustion of the adrenals results. Literally, the adrenals will atrophy, shrink and be unable to function properly. The symptoms of this stage of the GAS are:

- low blood sugar
- low blood pressure
- low body temperture
- no energy or endurance
- mental lethargy
- proneness to depression
- a general feeling of illness

Some people reading this list might recognize its strong correlation with the symptoms of thyroid deficiency. Adrenal-thyroid interdependencies are another mystery of the endocrine system that is still largely overlooked. If the adrenals are overburdened, the thyroid will also become sluggish. It appears that in order to give the adrenals a chance to rest, the thyroid slows down metabolism. The explanation for this is not certain, but it could involve the glucocorticoids. This is the endocrine relationship that is involved in CFIDS, fibromyalgia and the stress syndrome.

Many sufferers of CFIDS, fibromyalgia and general malaise syndrome recognize these symptoms. This adrenal exhaustion stage is marked by the adrenals' inability to produce cortisol. Adrenal exhaustion is difficult to determine clinically, but one of the advantages of the diagnosis of CFIDS is that researchers now have embraced the concept of subclinical adrenal weakness. A way has been found to test for this condition by drawing blood, from which a baseline cortisol level is determined and, immediately thereafter, the patient is injected with ACTH. Thirty minutes later, another blood sample is taken. If the cortisol levels do not at least double from the baseline number, adrenal exhaustion is indicated. In order to recover from such a condition, a patient must guard his adrenal reserve by maintaining proper nutrition, getting plenty of rest and reducing toxic encounters of all kinds—environmental and emotional.

Many alternative practitioners, knowing of the relationship of stress to CFIDS, have begun using DHEA to improve a patient's subjective sense of well-being. (Interestingly, DHEA appears to have improved thyroid function in laboratory rats.) No studies have been conducted yet to determine if the same effects pertain to humans as well. Because adrenal weakness also involves subclinically weak thyroid function, I have found that providing one grain of desiccated thyroid in conjunction with DHEA produces dramatic results, improving immune function, as well as lifting depression and enhancing the ability to cope.

THE SECOND MAGIC ACT

The perception of danger by an individual triggers a complex set of actions and reactions in the body that follow one another according to a predetermined script. This bodily response of distress involves a dramatic interplay of physiological events. To understand it, we must first look to the brain's structure.

Located in the lower part of the brain, the brain stem is

the most primitive structure upon which all other cerebral structures develop. It is the brain stem which contains the hypothalamus and the thalamus, two very important glands that determine how one reacts to incoming information. Attached to the brain stem are the deep interconnected structures that as a group make up what is called the limbic system. Within this area of the brain, one such structure called the amygdala causes the initial emotional reaction to environments and situations. Derived from the Greek word for almond, the amygdala is so named because of its shape.

A visual signal of threat (such as your child being attacked or a gun being pulled on you) travels first to the thalamus. The thalamus, recognizing the danger, signals the amygdala whether to react emotionally while simultaneously signaling the forebrain to analyze the situation. If the emotional response is great, the amygdala signals the release of epinephrine from the hypothalamus down the sympathetic nervous system, raising blood pressure, increasing heart rate, stimulating the liver and tissue to give up sugar (glucose) to the smooth muscles to prepare the body for "fight or flight." As the signals from the amygdala continue, the hypothalamus stimulates the pituitary to release ACTH from the adrenals to protect the body from the stress and strain and, in case of injury, to allow it to continue fighting or run, if necessary.

If the sustained background information the brain is receiving over a period of time is emotionally stressful, as might be the case if one is in living in an abusive home or crime-ridden neighborhood, the amygdala remains triggered, ready to respond to the slightest provocation. Firing the trigger would almost be a blessing in that it would release pent-up chemical responses. Unfortunately, many people learn to accommodate this level of stress continually—to their own detriment and eventual demise. If stressful jobs, abusive spouses, and neighborhood thugs don't kill them, cancer or some degenerative disease may.

Listed here are the physical effects that adrenaline production from the medulla has on an individual:

1) dilates the pupils

2) increases heart rate

3) increases blood pressure to speed the delivery of oxygen, glucose and hormones to target cells in the smooth muscles, heart and skeleton

4) decreases blood flow to organs not in use at the time, such as the stomach and colon

5) decreases kidney function and increases urine output

6) causes the liver to release stored glycogen which increases blood glucose levels

7) increases muscle strength and mental activity and acuity

8) causes bronchial dilation which moves carbon dioxide quickly out of the system and increases oxygen delivery into the bloodstream

9) and speeds up cellular metabolic rates by as much as 100%!

THE SAGA OF TWO SISTERS

May I introduce our heroine, Regina Rushes? Regina loves adrenaline, so much so that she voluntarily submits herself on a regular basis to life-threatening situations in her chosen field of employment. Regina is a professional race car driver.

Regina is in the sixth position in the 112th lap of a rather uneventful race (as far as the fans are concerned). The usual jockeying for position at speeds exceeding 190 miles per hour and cutting to the inside of curves banked at 30-40 degrees have proceeded without incident. That is until Axel Rod decides that the time to make his move has arrived. Seeing a likely slot by which to pass Regina on the next high-banked curve, he drops down from the high position, cuts across Regina's path and clips her front bumper. Regina's car begins to spin uncontrollably. This is what gets the fans to their feet. A collective gasp rises from the stands as the crowd stretches and strains to get a better view, their adrenals pumping in anticipation of impending disaster.

As the vehicle spins, tires squeal and the blue smoke of burning rubber envelopes her. Regina's hypothalamus, the "pit boss" of her body, is shouting orders and monitoring the process. Her hypothalamus (located deep within her brain above the pituitary), upon realizing the impact of Axel Rod's vehicle and her loss of control of the steering, screams orders into the headset of her brain. Instantaneously, excited messengers run down the length of Regina's central nervous system (excitatory blasts from hypothalamic neurons descend along her spinal cord) along the ganglia, stimulating the adrenal medulla, the sympathetic nervous system and the anterior pituitary. The anterior pituitary releases ACTH (adrenocorticotropin hormone) to the adrenal cortex as the pit crews scramble into action. The famous "fight or flight" response is initiated.

The sympathetic nervous system crew, or the catecolamines, as they prefer to call themselves, led by Epi (epinephrine) and Nora (norepinephrine), make fuel readily available by increasing the flow of blood to the liver and enhance sugar, fat and protein breakdown to provide fuel and amino acids to meet the need for the increased cellular activity of the muscles and brain. This increase in glycogen (sugar) stimulates the brain and increases Regina's mental acuity. It causes a sensation of the suspension of time, slowing every action down to a deliberate move. All the lessons she has experienced about similar situations seem to come to her automatically as her brain functions on overdrive for her survival.

Regina pumps the brakes to ensure that they will not lock up as she steers into the skid to prevent her vehicle from flipping. This activity is very intense. Regina is burning fuel (glucose) rapidly and generating heat in the process as she breaks into a sweat. Her bronchioles dilate to rid the body of the carbon dioxide created by her high sugar usage, making it easier for her to replenish herself with oxygen to help keep her conscious. From her adrenal cortex, ACTH has stimulated the release of steroid hormones, most notably the corticoids which act as anti-inflammatories. All of these responses are automatic; there is no thought of the process. Because Regina is trained to handle these types of situations, most of her reactions are modulated through higher hypothalamic control of catecholamine production. Her hypothalamus recognizes the danger but also acknowledges that it can be handled.

BAM!!!!! Race car number 35 slams broadside into Regina's car and pushes her across the green. As the spinning stops, the front axle bends obliquely, grinding her car to a halt. Regina releases her harness and pulls herself out the window of her "totaled" vehicle. She becomes aware of herself standing on the green with no discernible injuries, although her right wrist feels "floppy." She begins to realize that the threat has passed. Thick smoke drifts before her eyes as she turns her attention to the car that hit her and sees smoke billowing from under its hood. Through the haze she recognizes the car's number as that belonging to Randy Ratchett, her husband. She screams her husband's name as she runs to the smoking car. Randy is unconscious. Fearing that the car will burst into flames, Regina flails at Randy's harness to get him loose. She rips the buckle from the release and lifts her 185-pound husband through the window just as flames begin flickering under the dash. Her petite 110-pound frame drags her husband 25 feet from the vehicle before the crash team members arrive to assist her. Others race to the car with fire extinguishers.

Regina's reaction to her husband's accident was caused by a dramatic increase in epinephrine output giving her the strength and the courage to do the heroic. Both she and her husband suffered various injuries. Regina found she had a broken wrist and major contusions on the hips and thighs—Randy, a severe concussion. Although disappointed that they missed a planned skydiving event scheduled for the following weekend, they are cavalier about the necessary risks of their profession. In truth, they love the experience of having cheated death. It's a rush and, by golly, it makes them feel alive and incidentally—grateful. As flippant and crazy as Regina's frequent bouts with dangerous situations might sound, in reality, these are somewhat healthier adrenal experiences than those of Regina's sister living in the quiet suburbs of Baltimore.

Rosemary Ruin is Regina's younger sister. Rosemary is living in hell. It hasn't always been like this. Her husband, Dick, was a middle management executive for a company that went through the rigors of "downsizing" two and a half years ago. Dick was too old to be snatched up by a similar company because of his age and pre-existing heart condition and too over educated to gracefully accept a part-time stock boy position at the local hardware store with a supervisor 20 years his junior. He has taken up alcohol to numb his feelings of inadequacy. Rosemary is watching their savings dwindle in order to valiantly maintain their investment in a comfortable home in the suburbs. Dick has assured her he will be back at work soon, making the same kind of money he made before.

For not having "seen the handwriting on the wall" and being unable to face Rosemary's tears of frustration and anger, Dick has become more and more explosive, initially shouting and pushing, then escalating into serious abuse. All this has caused Dick to feel guilty and frustrated. He drinks to wind down. Very quickly his pattern turns to binge drinking. He is a belligerent drunk. He becomes increasingly more explosive and the cycle continues. As their second mortgage becomes five months overdue, they can no longer afford their health insurance. Bill collectors begin calling about their maxed-out credit cards. Rosemary's adrenals go into "overdrive." She wakes early between 2:30 and 4:00 a.m. every morning. Often her heart is pounding and she has difficulty taking a deep breath. After a particularly frightening episode, an emergency room doctor diagnoses her symptoms as an anxiety attack and hands her a bill for $520 (two and a half weeks wages) for sitting three hours in a waiting room to have an EKG and chem panel run and a $3\frac{1}{2}$ minute visit with the attending physician. She leaves with a prescription for Xanax. Increasingly, she finds herself drenched in sweat and, no, they are not hot flashes. Rosemary is only 39.

Rosemary is so fatigued by worry that she has become addicted to Excedrin and coffee to get her on her feet every day. One morning she notices a large walnut-shaped lump (swollen lymph node) under her jaw. Despite feeling sick and achy all the time, she can't miss work, so she drags herself through the motions. Every month is a struggle to make ends meet. She has to scrape change together to buy laundry detergent and toilet paper. She looks at herself in the mirror.

She looks like a used dishrag. She no longer takes the time to do her hair or put on makeup. She's too exhausted. She doesn't feel she has the energy to be social and if she had it her way, she would go to bed for a month. Depression is gnawing away at her emotional reserves.

Rosemary's adrenals are shot!! She has burned out her capacitors (depleted her adrenal reserves through hypertrophy) and blown a fuse or tripped a breaker (her glucolorticoids have risen so high as to inhibit insulin production and block the body's intake of fuel). The power source within her internal circuitry has been perilously depleted, if not entirely interrupted (she lacks vitality and her immune system is compromised if not thoroughly impaired). Hoping to restore some "juice" to her system, she seeks stimulation artificially through caffeine etc., to charge herself.

Both Regina's and Rosemary's DHEA levels decline naturally with age. During the crash and rescue, Regina's adrenals never moved within range of the *alarm phase*, as described in Dr. Seyle's theory. If research were done on Rosemary, we would probably find that her DHEA-DHEAS ratios started showing abnormally low levels as her symptoms moved into the *maladaptive phase*. Clinical evidence would show her DHEA levels as definitely depleted by the time she reaches the *exhaustion phase* of the GAS. This typically spells the onset of degenerative disease such as arthritis, cancer, cardiovascular disease, diabetes or immunodeficiency. It's only a matter of time before Rosemary's cascade of stress-related symptoms culminates in a catastrophic disease. Dangerously low DHEA levels are indicators of pathology. Which disease an individual develops is dependent on genetic predispositions and physiological weaknesses exacerbated by specific behaviors and environments.

Many people get addicted to adrenaline and the responses it creates in the body. They feel flat and dull unless there is some form of drama or terror in their lives to keep them on edge. Some of these adrenaline addictions are not as obvious as they are with our race car driving couple. Instead they are insidious and tragic.

CHINESE INTERPRETATION OF KIDNEY AND DHEA

The fundamentals of Traditional Chinese Medicine (TCM) useful in diagnosis and treatment are based on three concepts: the meridian system, the five element theory and the *yin-yang* theory. The TCM view of the human body is that there are 12 main meridians, five elements that are related to the forces of nature (earth, wood, fire, water and metal) and two basic characteristics of all things—*yin* and *yang*.

THE MERIDIANS

Meridians can be likened to electrical wiring or to a flowing river—they carry the body's energy, known as *chi*, from one area of the body to another. If a meridian is blocked due to injury or poor health, the *chi* cannot be delivered well to points beyond the blockage. This causes a form of imbalance called *deficiency* in those channels. Conversely, too much energy flooding the meridian, because it is not able to disperse its energy evenly along its path, causes another form of imbalance called *excess*.

The main meridians are named after the respective organ energy flow that they channel:
- heart
- small intestine
- liver
- gall bladder
- lung
- large intestine
- spleen (In TCM, the spleen meridian refers anatomically more to the functions of the pancreas as it is related to digestion and insulin production.)
- stomach
- pericardium or heart constrictor
- triple warmer
- kidney
- bladder

The "triple warmer" from the list above is a difficult concept to describe. It refers to the 3 centers of accumulation of *chi* to be dispersed throughout the body: the upper, middle and lower warmer. These centers of accumulation of *chi* are related to controlling the body's fluids.

1. The upper warmer represents the chest and relates to the ability to transport *chi* (energy) and blood to nourish various parts of the body.

2. The middle warmer relates to digestion and absorption.

3. The lower warmer relates to maintaining water metabolism and the excretion of urine.

THE FIVE ELEMENTS

The meridians and organs are related to each other through the five element theory with each meridian and its related organs associated with one of the five elements;

- <u>fire</u> element is associated with the heart, small intestine, pericardium and triple warmer
- <u>earth</u> element is associated with the stomach and spleen/pancreas
- <u>wood</u> element is associated with the liver and gall bladder
- <u>metal</u> element is associated with the lungs and large intestine
- <u>water</u> element is associated with the kidneys and bladder.

YIN AND YANG

Integral to Chinese thought is that all things—including medical conditions—have *yin* and *yang* characteristics. Yin and yang can be defined as interdependent opposites. Yin connotes passive, deep, dark, down, cold, internal, and deficient, while yang characteristics are active, surface, light, up, hot, external, and excess. Externally, the perverse energies of wind, heat, fire, humidity, dryness and cold attack the meridians and manifest on the exterior of the body (e.g. rashes, flushing, pustules, sweat) and are considered yang disorders. The seven passions—also considered perverse energies if experienced in unbalanced ways—attack the interior of the body. These passions are joy, apprehension, anger, reflection (or rumination), sadness, anguish and fear. They will cause internal manifestations of yin disorders (e.g. hypoglycemia, anemia, CFIDS). It is the qualities of the attack of these perverse

Five Elements

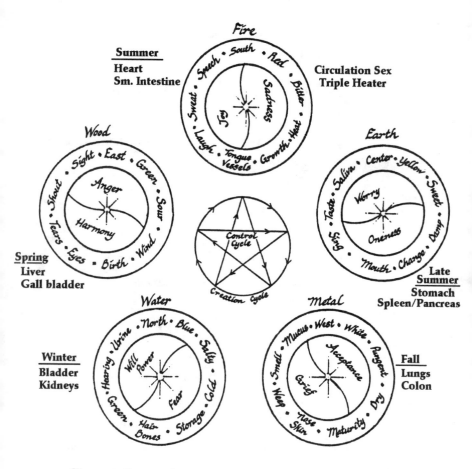

The creation cycle, represented by the circle moving in a clockwise direction, has easy-to-remember sequences based on traditional expressions of their abilities.

> **Fire** produces earth (ashes);
> **earth** produces metal (iron ore);
> **metal** produces water (in that gold, for example, can affect its ionization for purity);
> **water** produces wood (in the sense that water makes plant life possible);
> and **wood** produces fire (in that wood is fuel for fire).

The control, or destruction cycle, represented by the five-point star in the center is expressed in a similar manner.

Fire subjugates metal (fire melts metal);
metal subjugates wood (an axe fells a tree);
wood subjugates earth (trees/plants discourage erosion);
earth subjugates water (earth obstructs water flow
and absorbs water);
water subjugates fire (water extinguishes fire).

Notice the placement of attributes, seasons, paired organs and emotions associated with the five elements. Look at the diagram circularly in a clockwise fashion to follow the creation cycle. For the destruction or control cycle, look across the central circle following in the direction pointed out by the straight arrows that make up the star.

---

energies affecting meridian flows—and their interactions with one another—that in their combinations give Chinese diagnostic terminology its exotic-sounding descriptions (like deficient kidney yin, liver fire rising, cold damp spleen).

THE KIDNEY MERIDIAN

The five element theory provides guidelines as to the qualities and characteristics of each meridian. Let's focus on the kidney meridian. The kidney meridian refers anatomically to both the kidneys and the adrenal glands. In TCM, discussion of the kidneys naturally assumes adrenal interaction.

Much of the ancient Chinese understanding of the functions and characteristics of the kidney meridian has been verified through modern medical techniques. Recently published clinical findings regarding the benefits of DHEA to adrenal function strongly support TCM's theories, particularly the effect on the body as a whole of the kidney meridian's energy.

As mentioned previously, specific characteristics have been assigned to each of the 12 meridians—the result of observations made over thousands of years and applied through the five element theory. For example, the kidney meridian is paired with the bladder meridian. They are both ruled by the water element. Winter is the season that is associated with the kidney/bladder meridians and is the time when the most care must be taken to protect them, as cold attacks the kidneys and bladder. It is believed that to conserve the kidneys in the winter, individuals should sleep longer hours. Being in harmony with seasonal variances in daylight and night ensures a good supply of kidney vitality for the work and activity of the longer daylight hours of Spring. Appropriate rest, including sleep and restful holidays or "down time" is very important for conserving kidney energy.

The five element theory has a creation (generation) and a destruction (control) cycle. The creation cycle involves support and harmony; the destruction cycle involves attack and disharmony. In the creation phase of the cycle, the meridian that supports the kidneys is the lung meridian. The kidney meridian goes on to support the spleen/pancreas and stomach meridians. When out of harmony and in the destruction cycle, the kidney meridian attacks the heart meridian. If you experience a sudden, frightening event, the emotion associated with the kidney meridian, fear, is experienced and the kidney/adrenals production of adrenaline causes the heart to beat rapidly. Another aspect of this attack upon the heart meridian by the kidney meridian involves the regulation of blood pressure. It is a well-documented phenomenon that the kidneys' failure to regulate blood pressure properly puts a great deal of strain on the heart, a critical factor in cardiovascular disease and stroke.

The taste associated with the kidney meridian is salty. Sodium, or salt, is necessary for the heart to maintain a steady and strong beat. However, sodium in excess will cause the body to retain water which weaken the kidneys, thereby increasing blood pressure and straining the heart. The kidney meridian also controls the lower back and the knees. Low back pain, or lumbago, can be the first sign of kidney problems. The knee connection is understandable if one considers its relationship to the gastrocnemius muscle (the calf of the leg). It is the first skeletal muscle to give up sugar in the fight and flight response of an adrenal "rush." Often, one becomes weak in the knees and is unable to stand after reacting to a frightening event.

Blue/black is the color associated with the kidney/bladder meridians. Dark circles under the eyes and a gray ashen look in complexion are signs of depleted kidneys. Fear is the emotion. Groaning and sighing are the sounds a person with deficient kidney energy often makes ("a whiner"). Strong, thick, shiny hair, strong teeth resistant to cavities and strong bones are signs of good kidney condition. The organ which the kidneys "open into" are the ears—hearing loss in the elderly and middle ear infections (otitis media) in children are (as described in Chinese medicine) signs of deficiency in the kidney meridian.

The kidney meridian is the only meridian that is described as having both yin and yang qualities. Kidney yin is the "essence of vitality" while kidney yang contains and regulates the kidney yin. These yin and yang qualities must be in harmony to maintain the proper functioning of the kidneys. The ability of the kidney yang to contain and properly direct the kidney yin is the primary task of this meridian.

Note the specific characteristics of various kidney meridian functions within TCM:

1. *storing essence* and *dominating reproduction, growth and development*

2. *producing marrow* [The Chinese concept of *marrow* is broader than the spongy matter that forms the central structure of a number of bones of the body and which manufactures blood cells. In TCM, *marrow* includes the structures of the central nervous system (like the spine and brain) and the brain is referred to as the *sea of marrow.*]

3. *dominating body fluid*

4. *grasping chi* [This unique concept describes the kidney meridian's function of pulling the *energy* of respiration down into the body to regulate *chi* flow.]

Let's take a deeper look at the separate functions performed by the kidney meridian as they are conceptualized within the Chinese system and understood in Western terms.

1.) storing "essence" and dominating reproduction, growth and development

The kidneys are the storehouse of the body's most vital energies, *chi*, and is responsible for the source of life. The original energy or innate energy——encouraging an individual to grow and thrive——is first inherited from the parents. It is called *yuan chi* and is what might be called constitution, as in "he has a strong constitution." As the individual grows, the *chi* is further influenced by diet and lifestyle practices and is called *acquired chi*. The *yuan chi* and the *acquired chi* combined are referred to as *jing*. This *kidney jing* function is described as *conception made possible by the power of the parental jing*; growth into maturity is the *flourishing of jing* and the decline into old age is the *weakening of jing*.

The *Neiching* is a 4,000-year-old manuscript considered

the foundation text of Chinese medicine. In it, the Yellow Emperor and his chief physician, Su Wen, discuss kidney energy. Their exchange offers a remarkably similar description of what modern researchers tell us about DHEA and aging. A translated portion of their discussion is quoted here:

"The kidneys energy of a woman becomes in abundance at the age of 7, her baby teeth begin to be replaced by permanent ones and her hair begins to grow longer. At the age of 14, a woman will begin to have menstruation, her conception meridian begins to flow, and the energy in her connective meridian begins to grow in abundance, and she begins to have menstruation which is the reason why she is capable of becoming equal to an average adult, and for that reason, her last tooth begins to grow with all other teeth completed.

At the age of 28, tendons and bones become hard, the hair grows to the longest, and the body is in the top conditions. At the age of 35, the bright Yang meridians begin to weaken with the result that her complexion starts to look withered, and her hair begins to fall off. At the age of 42, the three Yang meridians begin to weaken with the result that her complexion starts to look withered, and her hair begins to turn gray. At the age of 49, the energy of the conception meridian becomes in deficiency, the energy of the connective meridian becomes weakened and scanty, the sex energy becomes exhausted, and menstruation stops with the result that her body becomes old and she cannot become pregnant any longer.

As to man, his kidney energy becomes in abundance, his hair begins to grow longer, and his teeth begin to change at the age of 8. At the age of 16, his kidneys energy becomes even more abundant, his sex energy begins to arrive, he is full of semen that he can ejaculate. When he has a sexual intercourse with woman, he can have children.

At the age of 24, the kidneys energy of a man becomes equal to an average adult with strong tendons and bones, his last tooth begins to grow with all other teeth completed. At the age of 32, all tendons, bones,. and muscles are already fully grown. At the age of 42, the kidneys energy begins to weaken, hair begins to fall off, and teeth begin to wither. At the age of 48, a weakening and exhaustion of Yang energy begins to take place in the upper region with the result that all parts of the body begin to grow old. At the age of 64, hair and teeth are gone."

Compare their discussion with what is known about DHEA:

• fetal levels fall off dramatically after birth

• a marked surge in secretion begins again near age 7, apparently preparing the body for puberty

• levels continue to increase to their highest levels in the late 20's to early 30's

• levels steadily decline from age 30, plummeting to their lowest levels (10-15% of young adult levels) from age 70 on.

Many alternative practitioners believe that an adrenally weak mother will drain the adrenal outputs of her fetus. Fetuses are known to produce DHEA. Umbilical cord levels were measured in one study of 74 newborns. The study reported extremely wide variances in individual newborn DHEA levels from 21.8 to 267. Extremely low DHEA levels were reported primarily in male newborns even though the mean averages of the girls (133.7) were similar to the mean averages of the boys (133.4) (de Peretti et. al., 1978). These wide variances in individual production of DHEA are important. A fetus' adrenals, forced to produce enough hormones for itself and its mother, will quickly become overtaxed. This stress upon the fetus increases glucocorticoid production and, without enough DHEA to block the negative effects of glucocorticoid excess (DHEA levels decline dramatically within the first month after birth to 0.2 - 28 mcg/dl), the child will become prone to food sensitivities, repeated infections and irritability.

In Chinese medicine when the kidney energy is deficient, one will experience mental lethargy. The initial sign of an individual suffering deficient kidney *chi* is the occurrence of middle ear infections (*otitis media*). In the U.S., ear infections account for nearly 80% of all pediatric visits for children between the ages of 3 months to 3 years. Boys account for a high percentage of the sufferers. Many mothers come to recognize that the child is "allergic" to dairy products. This sensitivity displays itself because the high fat content and the amino acid profile of cow's milk is radically different from human milk. A child's immune system, weakened by this adrenal drain, cannot withstand this assault. The intolerance for dairy products produces inflammatory reactions that stimulate mucous production. A weakened immune system cannot protect the child against a virulent bacteria like streptococcus. Remember, the organ the kidney meridian *opens into* is the ear.

KIDNEY DEPLETION AND ATTENTION DEFICIT DISORDER

Recently, there has been a dramatic increase in the diagnoses of the nebulous Attention Deficit Disorder (ADD). Many times the condition can be traced to an earlier history of middle ear infections. ADD and its treatment protocol have become very controversial. Statistics suggest boys suffer with ADD 4 to 1 more than girls. In the past 10 years, there has been a phenomenal rise in the occurrence of ADD in the U.S., far more than in any other Western nation. In February of 1996, the United Nations published a document warning of the over 600% rise in U.S. diagnosis of this condition. Apparently, 3 - 5% of all school children (12% of all boys 6-14 years old) in the U.S. are on a methamphetamine-like drug, because the standard treatment protocol is a prescription for Ritalin.

What exactly is Attention Deficit Disorder? There appear to be no pathophysiological markers used to make the diagnosis, although a study conducted by Nottlemen et. al., reported in the *Journal of Pediatrics* in 1987, showed that DHEAS levels were found to be low in children reported to be hyperactive and with "acting out" behaviors. These characteristics now fall under the general ADD label. The report went on to say that levels of another adrenal androgen, androstenedione (which is a breakdown product of DHEA), were significantly high. Apparently, DHEA was being pushed on into the next metabolic phase rather than being conjugated out of the system as DHEAS. This is not to suggest that parents seek out DHEA for their ADD or hyperactive children, but to caution them about the long-term effects of Ritalin. Because its chemical structure and action further depletes adrenals, the choice of this treatment is potentially more damaging to a system that is already disturbed, even if it does provide some temporary relief in the symptoms of the disorder.

The standard protocol of Ritalin treatment is in itself highly suspect. The term ADD is applied to a constellation of symptoms which are very vague and could pertain to any child who would rather be outside playing than be cooped up in a room. Ritalin is generally given by the school nurse only when the child is in school, not during weekends and vacations. The inability to concentrate and remain settled is more a symptom of boredom and confinement. Rather than being the child's fault, it is the inability of the school system to address the natural activity levels of a significant population of children. The desire to contain all children within a sedentary teaching environment should be reexamined. Because of budget cuts and overcrowding, the practice of maintaining control of the classroom by pharmacological means has put the school's interests ahead of the needs and, potentially, the health of its students.

2.) Producing "marrow"

The Chinese believe that the kidneys are the *master of bone* and *generate marrow*. They also believe that *marrow* is in communication with the brain and that the brain is the *sea of marrow*. When the kidneys are full of energy, one is energetic, clear thinking and one's bones are hard and strong.

Ergocalciferol is a steroidal form of vitamin D synthesized by ultraviolet light irradiating the cholesterol in the skin. It is transformed into the bioactive form of the vitamin by the kidneys. The kidneys then put the active vitamin D into circulation. The parathyroid glands take vitamin D out of the blood in order to utilize calcium and phosphorus for the laying of proper bone apatates, the building blocks of bone. DHEA has been found to improve bone density in postmenopausal women (Spector et. al., 1991).

The kidneys are also said to *produce blood* in Chinese medicine. In Western terms, the formation of blood cells is called *hemopoiesis* and is known to take place in the marrow where both red and white blood cell production occurs. Marrow, as the term is used in Western medicine, is the internal soft tissue present in some bones, particularly in the vertebrae, ribs, sternum, skull, pelvis and the "long" bones of the humerus of the arm and the femur of the leg. Blood cells are formed in the marrow through the production and differentiation of stem cells which permanently reside there. One type forms the red cells, another the white and another the platelets. The white cells, or leukocytes, go on to differentiate into various immune factors such as monocytes, neutrophils, eosinophils, monocytes, macrophages, lymphocytes and the like. Lymphocytes go on to the lymph structures and the thymus to become specialized immune factors including T-killer cells, T-helper cells (CD-4), T-suppressor cells (CD-8) and cytokines. The decline of kidney energy has a significant bearing on the body's defense mechanism against disease.

DHEA, in numerous clinical studies, has been shown to improve the production and effectiveness of T-cell factors, as well as stimulating the production of another important immune factor, interleukin-2 (IL-2). IL-2 stimulates T-cell growth, particularly CD-4 cells, and stimulates the secretion of antibodies. There are very important functions to a competent immune system. It is immunosuppression which is the hallmark of diseases like AIDS and SLE that display weak or non-existent IL-2 and T-cell factor production.

DHEA also appears to improve the liver's production of

Insulin-like Growth Factor-1 (IGF-1), often causing the thymus to be restored to its normal size and function (Yen et. al., 1995). With age or under stressful conditions, the thymus begins to shrink. This shrinkage impairs the thymus' ability to produce all of its immune factors. DHEA's ability to keep us resistant to illness may be linked to IGF-1 production.

Finally, the kidneys make another hormone named erythropoietin that is directly responsible for the marrow's production of red blood cells (RBC's). Red blood cells are necessary for the transportation of oxygen throughout the body. Generally, erythropoietin is called into action only when surrounding air pressure, such as that found at high altitude, makes circulating adequate amounts of oxygen difficult. By increasing the number of RBC's with erythropoietin, the body can thereby ensure adequate oxygen to nourish the cells and maintain awareness.

DHEA AND "THE SEA OF MARROW"

Perhaps the effect most appreciated by those who have used supplemental DHEA is its neurosteroid potential to improve mood and perception. In laboratory studies of rats on DHEA, results have shown significant uptake of DHEA in their amygdala, hippocampus, thalamus, midbrain and frontal cortex. These brain structures are responsible for interpreting environmental stimuli before analyzing what responses are most appropriate. By analogy, DHEA's function in humans suggests it has a calming effect as a neurosteroid on otherwise anxiety-producing emotional responses to stressors, particularily in people prone to panic attacks. On the other hand, DHEA seems to have an antidepressant effect in individuals with excessive glucocorticoid production. Elevated glucocorticoid production is associated with Alzheimer's Disease, as well as fibromyalgia, CFIDS, SLE, AIDS and other still unlabelled autoimmune disorders. In other words, DHEA seems to alleviate both depression and anxiety. Depression, pessimism and social isolation are three critical factors contributing to the onset and progression of disease.

Social isolation itself, as reported in 1987 in *Science Magazine* "...is as significant to mortality rates as smoking, high blood pressure, high cholesterol, obesity and lack of physical exercise." Based on a Swedish study published in 1993, isolation is harder on men than on women. It also showed that men in isolation were 2-3 times more likely to die as were men with close social ties. If DHEA can improve mood, its supplementation might encourage the creation of social ties for individuals otherwise isolated because of anxiety or depression.

ALZHEIMER'S DISEASE

The mental isolation characteristic of suspected Alzheimer's Disease patients could be minimized with DHEA supplementation. Alzheimer's disease (AD) is estimated to afflict 4 million Americans. AD is another mysterious illness that has no known cause. It is marked by mental loss, confusion, depression and fatigue. The tragedy of AD is that the illness creates a wide circle of victims including family and friends who attempt to care for their ailing loved one. These family/ friend caretakers, especially with in-home care, are often severely stressed both emotionally and physically.

Once again significant decreases in DHEA levels have been noted in suspected AD sufferers——as much as a 48% decrease in normal age-relative DHEA levels. Because of these findings and the evidence of past studies in which participants on DHEA claimed great subjective improvements in mood and energy, clinical studies are now underway at the National Institute of Mental Health (NIMH) to examine DHEA in relation to Alzheimer's Disease.

3.) Dominating water metabolism

The mineralocorticoid aldosterone, an antidiuretic hormone, is secreted by the adrenals and controls the excretion and retention of water. Aldosterone is a hormone that regulates plasma salts (including sodium and potassium), blood pressure and blood volume. The balance between sodium and potassium is critical. Sodium, potassium, magnesium and calcium have electrical charges and are therefore called electrolytes. They act as the "gatekeepers" of every cell in the body, allowing or inhibiting the exchange of their respective electrical charges through these cellular gates. If aldosterone is functioning correctly, the electrolyte levels within the blood and tissues ensure fluids and proper cellular metabolism essential to good health. Stress and chronic degenerative conditions are often marked by abnormal sodium/potassium ratios.

Edema is the retention of water by tissue, usually around the ankles. Paradoxial edema is a condition that alternative practitioners use to describe a symptom which is typical in adrenally weak individuals. Its appearance is associated with the maladaptive stage of the GAS. The maladaptive phase of the stress syndrome involves excessive glucocorticoid production. When glucocorticoids are elevated, so is aldosterone production. This increase in aldosterone causes the retention of sodium and the excretion of potassium through the kidneys. Diuretics are not recommended by alternative practitioners in these cases, since they can exacerbate the condition. *Moderate* but consistent water intake dramatically diminishes conditions of paradoxial edema. Potassium support is given at this time (also contrary to conventional medical practice). The "folk" cure of apple cider vinegar and honey in water is a good way to get the moderate amounts of potassium needed to offset the condition. The general weakened adrenal condition of the population is the reason such products as *kM*® made such an impact with consumers. DHEA and its ability to alleviate the impact of excess glucocorticoids could be of use in restoring proper aldosterone function.

In Chinese medicine, a craving for salt and salty things is a sign of kidney weakness. Cravings for things like salted potato chips, french fries and peanuts (or lacing your food with tamari/soy sauce) are signs of adrenal weakness. Rats with adrenal insufficiency are known to spontaneously increase the amount of their salt intake. TCM employs a form of physiognomy, the reading of facial and bodily features, as a diagnostic tool. A person with swollen puffy bags under the eyes—retention of water associated with high salt intake— is a sign the kidneys are under stress and will in turn *attack* the heart (destruction cycle of the five element system). Dark blue/black or gray circles under the eyes are definitely a sign of stress and generally one of the first, along with lumbago, of serious kidney/adrenal insufficiency.

4.) Grasping chi

This concept can be explained by two functions involving

the lungs that the kidneys and adrenals can perform. Remember, in the *creation* cycle of the five element system, the lungs *nourish* the kidneys.

Angiotensin-1 is a small protein molecule produced by the liver that circulates through the blood. It is ready to go into action if there is excess blood loss or a drop in blood pressure, as with cases of chronic hypoadrenia (adrenal insufficiency). As angiotensin-1 circulates in the blood, the lungs convert it into angiotensin-2 which causes a contraction, a tightening of the vascular walls, thereby raising blood pressure. Angiotensin-2 will then go on to stimulate the adrenals to produce aldosterone, for regulating blood pressure back into normal range.

Many people with weak adrenals complain of "the black whirlies." Scientifically, it is termed *vertigo*. This condition usually occurs when an individual suddenly rises to his feet after sitting for a time. The room seems to spin and they have a sense of loss of balance and reach out to catch themselves as their vision goes black momentarily. Most individuals "come to" within split seconds, while a few actually pass out. This is a typical sign of adrenal weakness. These "black whirlies" are the effect of the slow responses of exhausted adrenal and kidney hormone controls trying to maintain proper blood pressure.

Hypoadrenia is accompanied by remarkably low blood pressure, so low in fact that you will get comments from the nurses taking it like "Gee, what's your secret? You must be doing something right." When you go to a gym at the age of 45, and your heart rate is near 60, coupled with blood pressure of 90/60, the new personal trainer asks you if you are a marathon runner. You smile wide, because it required exhaustive effort on your part just to ruminate over the decision of whether to join a gym or not.

TAKING CARE OF THE KIDNEYS

Hopefully, we were born into life with a strong kidney *yuan chi* from our parents. Exercise, rest, moderation in lifestyle and eating right will replenish our kidney energy and give us strong *jing*. With strong *jing*, we will be blessed with good *shen*. The closest concept we have to *shen* is "spirit." Some of the abundant *jing* generated by healthy kidneys will, upon entering the heart meridian (if it is traveling the proper route of the creative cycle), turn to *shen*. Good *shen*, or spirit, is most noticeable in a person's eyes and voice. With vitality shining through the eyes and resonation in the voice, the feelings one encounters in such individuals are strength, compassion and kindness. Individuals with good *shen* tend not to get ill as much or as often and, generally, they are more at peace with life.

In Chinese medicine, sudden shock, prolonged stress or illness, a sedentary lifestyle and poor diet can combine to drain kidney energy. This depletion of the kidneys will hasten the classic signs of aging: hearing and hair loss, a weakened, frail condition overall and brittle bones. If kidney *jing* weakens too far, causing a complete *separation of kidney yin and yang*— we die.

Dr. Selye's GAS theory and the findings of DHEA research appear to corroborate these ancient medical concepts.

THE HEART

Estrogen has a protective role in preventing atherosclerosis and resultant cardiovascular disease. Estrogen allows blood vessels to remain flexible and protects the arteries from the accumulation of cholesterol. Before menopause, it is the production of this hormone in women that is credited for their reduced incidence of heart attack and stroke. Due to ovarian shutdown of its production after menopause, a woman's risk of heart disease is equal to a man's. Testosterone plays a role in a man's higher risk of stroke and heart attack and its supplementation in a woman also increases her risk.

Most of the studies on cardiovascular disease (CVD) have been conducted on men. In the studies that have been conducted on women, DHEA appeared to increase insulin resistance not shown in studies on men. Insulin resistance is a critical factor in heart disease. It is the inability to move sugar efficiently out of the bloodstream and into the energy-producing cycles of the body. It causes a rise in the sugar to be put away in the body as fat. The increase in fat can lead to obesity. There is a strong link between DHEA and this health-threatening pattern which creates a vicious cycle. High DHEAS levels have been shown to cause increased androgenic effects (including increased abdominal fat accumulation) which can lead to hyperinsulinemia. Hyperinsulinemia is characterized by elevated levels of insulin in the blood caused by insulin resistance of the tissues in not allowing insulin to carry sugar into the cell for energy production. This leads to a decline in a certain blood factor called serum hormone binding globulin (SHBG). SHBG acts to bind hormones to proteins in the blood to move them efficiently throughout the system. Without it, testosterone is left to circulate freely, thereby increasing visceral fat accumulation. The whole process is then repeated.

For men, there appears to be a strong relationship between DHEA/DHEAS levels and the occurrence of myocardial infarction (MI). In a retrospective study, serum levels of DHEAS were compared between a group of 49 men who had suffered myocardial infarction before the age of 56 and its age-matched control group. DHEAS levels were reported to be significantly lower in those who had suffered MI than in those who had not (Mitchell et. al., 1994). In a study published in the *New England Journal of Medicine* in 1986, DHEAS was reported to be significantly lower in men with a history of heart disease. In fact, those with low levels of DHEAS were 3.3 times more likely to die of heart disease than those with normal DHEAS levels (Barrett-Conner et. al., 1986).

In short, the research strongly suggests that, for men, DHEA supplementation can be of great benefit in the prevention of CVD. However, for postmenopausal women DHEA supplementation can substantially increase their risk.

The stronger proponents of DHEA supplementation are men. This fact must be taken into account. They cite remarkable experiences with the substance. A woman's hormone system is much more sensitive to the androgen production potential of DHEA, with more than 90% of her androgens being produced by her adrenal cortexes. It has been demonstrated in studies that the increase of androgen hormone levels in women as a result of relatively low doses of DHEA supplementation can be as much as 200%.

Inappropriate DHEA supplementation, especially in women, can cause acne, deepening of the voice, balding and excessive growth of facial hair (hirsutism). These side effects are not appreciated by or in women. They bespeak of potentially dangerous alterations in hormonal balances.

DHEA AND THE IMMUNE SYSTEM

The thymus is a mysterious pinkish-gray endocrine gland that sits behind the breastbone and above the heart. This gland is integral to the body's immunological defense system. At birth, the thymus weighs approximately 13 grams. Growth is rapid during the first two years, then slows down, so that it weighs about 30 gm. at puberty. After that, depending on the circumstances, it may begin to get fatty and atrophy. It was discovered that young people killed in accidents had remarkably larger thymuses than those who had died of chronic disease. Some researchers have reported that the thymus can shrink up to 50% per day from a severe disease or injury. Keep in mind that, as a part of the endocrine "web," the thymus does not act independently.

A reduction in the size and mass of the thymus gland is known as *thymic involution*. Over time, some shrinking of the thymus is considered normal, however there is evidence that stress (because of excessive adrenal output) accelerates the process. Chronic elevated glucocorticoids will cause this shrinkage, impairing critical T-cell function. A dramatic depletion of T-cells is one of the factors that moves an HIV patient towards full-blown AIDS. For the thymus to retain its integrity, it requires growth hormone (GH). GH is what causes our bodies to grow and mature by stimulating bone, cartilage and muscle development, as well as growth of other tissues throughout the body. In a growing body, GH is responsible for increasing the size and number of all cells. In a mature body, GH stimulates protein synthesis and muscle growth while encouraging the body to use up fat stores. It is fundamental to repairing damaged tissues, bone and cartilage. GH is also critical in keeping the thymus plump. Pituitary GH output steadily declines after puberty. GH is generally not produced in a body after the age of 50. To back up the pituitary output of GH, the body produces in the liver (and other tissue sites) a substance called Insulin-like Growth Factor (IGF), the liver being the major source. To date, there are two types of IGF— IGF-1 and IGF-2. DHEA has been shown to stimulate the production of IGF-1 which reverses shrinkage through thymic cell proliferation. The reversal of thymus shrinkage maintains T-helper cell (CD-4) production (McCoy, 1993). This capability of DHEA holds astounding possibilities for HIV-positive individuals. If the thymus can be maintained and output of critical CD-4 cells sustained, HIV may be inhibited from progressing into AIDS.

Arenal insufficiency should be suspected in AIDS patients. Both cytomegalovirus (CMV) and mycobacterium avium-intracellulare, a bacterial infection that resembles tuberculosis, regularly involve the adrenal glands. Cases of *Cryptococcus,* a parasitic fungal infection typical to AIDS patients, as well as Karposi's sarcoma, have reported adrenal involvement. Treatment of cryptoccoccus with DHEA was found to be successful among AIDS-infected lab mice, significantly reducing fungal colonies. The study reports a dramatic increase in immunosuppressor cells (CD-8) in the DHEA-treated mice (Rasmussen et. al., 1995). Standard laboratory tests are not definitive in measuring general adrenal weaknesses. However, a unique test sometimes administered to CFIDS patients to determine adrenal reserves can be performed on patients with other immunosuppression diseases like AIDS. Testing for DHEAS levels could also prove helpful. However, it must be understood that the natural diurnal rhythms of DHEA cause levels to be higher in the morning. Having DHEA/DHEAS levels checked at the same time, every time, is more accurate in determining actual levels.

My personal experiences with HIV and AIDS patients tend to support these research findings. Treating AIDS holistically is hinged on proactive lifestyle management including a good diet, reducing stress through meditation and yoga, and no drugs, including what some consider is one of the least harmful of drugs, marijuana. Marijuana can have a side effect of provoking feelings of anxiety known as "paranoia" and stimulating stressful "fight or flight" output of catecholamines. Marijuana also causes a hypoglycemic reaction as a part of its "high." Hypoglycemia is one of the most severe and entirely preventable stressors the body can endure. Reducing stress through lifestyle management extends HIV status long past prognostic projections. Research suggests DHEA could play a critical role. DHEA levels can be positively enhanced by stress reduction. Studies conducted on Transcendental Meditation (TM) practitioners proved that their DHEAS levels were significantly higher than among non-practicing controls. The controls were individuals who had the same dietary regime as the TM practitioners to eliminate any disparity caused by dietary influences. The stress-alleviating capability of a meditation practice was affirmed by the increase in natural DHEA outputs in the study's meditating participants (Glaser et. al., 1991).

SYSTEMIC LUPUS ERYTHEMATOSUS

Cytokines, also produced in the thymus, are a class of immune messengers that secrete chemical messages between immune cells. These messages modulate the immune response. The most well-known cytokine is interferon. Other cytokines are of a group called interleukins (IL). DHEA has been shown to stimulate production of these immune factors.

A deficiency of IL-2 is a common feature of systemic lupus erythematosus (SLE). While the reason is unknown at this time, DHEA appears to improve IL-2 production. This is very important news for sufferers of the autoimmune disease SLE (Suzuki et. al., 1995 and van Vollenhoven et. al., 1994). DHEA also appears to protect the kidneys from hemolytic anemia and SLE-triggered kidney destruction caused by increased amounts of proteins in the bloodstream of advanced cases of SLE (Regelson et. al., 1988).

ARTHRITIS

Arthritis, an inflammation of the joints and surrounding tendons, ligaments and cartilage, is one of the oldest known afflictions to cripple mankind. There are three basically common forms of the condition: *osteoarthritis*, *gout*, and *rheumatoid arthritis* (RA). Although paleological evidence of osteoarthritis has been found in human skeletons over 50,000 years old, rheumatoid arthritis was first found dating from the 16th century and emerging in Europe. The cause of RA is unknown and it has been classified as an autoimmune disease. Arthritis and diffuse "arthritic pain" are typically part of the symptomatology of autoimmune diseases. RA afflicts women three times more often than men. Besides being a very painful condition, it causes gross deformities of the joints it attacks. DHEA levels are reported to be low in individuals suffering from RA and are reported to be even lower after corticosteroid treatment (Sambrook et. al., 1988). Raising DHEA levels is known to improve thymic immune factors (CD-4, CD-8, IL-2 and IL-4) related to the body's ability to fight autoimmune diseases.

The beneficial effects in the maintenance of the immune system could be linked to a breakdown product of DHEA. In the skin and the brain, DHEA breaks down to androstenediol (AED). In tests conducted on virally infected mice, AED was found to be 10,000 times more effective than DHEA in stimulating thymic immune responses (Loria et. al., 1993). These responses are protective because they increase the ability of the infected animal to cope with the infection. Neither AED nor DHEA was shown to have direct antiviral or antibacterial capabilities. However, it seems AED can be used as a preventive therapy in protecting the host from the ravages of the infection, if not the infection itself.

CANCER

At the turn of this century, 1 in 35 Americans contracted cancer. Current cancer risk statistics are shocking. It is estimated now that 1 in 3 Americans will develop the disease (American Cancer Society, 1993). With less than 5% of cancers considered hereditary, melanoma and childhood leukemia making up the bulk of those cases, the risk of contracting it is obviously due to controllable factors.

Tobacco use is the leading cause of cancer deaths among both men and women with nearly 150,000 cases a year reported. Twenty percent of those cases are the result of the passive smoke exposure of non-smokers. Some 425,000 cases of lung disease and related illnesses linked to cigarette smoking are reported annually.

The rampant increase in our exposure to pesticides, herbicides, hormones and toxic compounds in food, water and air (even in tobacco products themselves) has occurred since the Industrial Revolution. Tons of radioactive and petrochemical waste are being "deposited" around the nation annually. The introduction of large quantities of chemicals and toxins of increasing complexity and undreamed-of combinations into our environment, generally, and into our bodies, particularly, can be correlated directly with the dramatic rise in the morbidity of cancer and other diseases.

Approximately half of this nation's population consistently breathe polluted air. Due to fossil fuel burning, deforestation and ocean pollution, carbon dioxide levels of the atmosphere have risen 15% and carbon monoxide 10% since 1950. Carbon monoxide with its high affinity for hemoglobin is able to displace biologically healthy O_2 oxygen in the blood. Proper oxygen levels within the blood are important to maintaining blood pH and correct cellular metabolic activity. Healthy cellular metabolism of oxygen is a significant key to cancer prevention.

Western civilization's love affair with unbridled *techno-ability* is reaping its victims. Many consider these conditions a necessary sacrifice for the amazing way we live these days, that is, until they or their loved ones are about to be "harvested."

Joseph W. Cullen, Ph.D., of the Division of Cancer Prevention Control at the National Cancer Institute in Bethesda, Maryland says "...cancer is largely an avoidable disease when adequate preventive measures are taken." According to the National Academy of Sciences, 60% of all cancers in women and 40% of all cancers in men are related to dietary and nutritional factors. The onset of cancer is probably a result of a combination of different factors that, in conjunction, trigger the development of the disease.

In simple terms, there are two types of cancer-causing elements that can be distinguished—*inductors* and *promoters*. Inductors, or initiators, are usually toxic compounds we encounter such as tobacco smoke, environmental pollution, pesticides, heavy metals, radioactive materials, industrial chemicals and aflatoxins. Inductors are not limited to toxic compounds. Circumstances that create toxic conditions like free radicals or radiation from the sun, even hormones, particularly estrogen, are also considered inductors. A promoter causes further cellular damage allowing cancer cells to continue their abnormal growth. A poor diet and stress are the greatest but entirely controllable cancer promoters.

ABOUT CANCER

Every cell in the body has the potential of becoming cancerous. In fact, on a daily basis many do. If the body's immune system has been damaged or overstressed, the ability of the body to slough off these cancerous cells is diminished. Cancer occurs when a cell's metabolism is affected in such a way as to cause a change in the cell's metabolic process, resulting in a growth pattern that breaks free of the normal genetically coded pattern. (This errant metabolic process is the opposite to that of normal tissue and causes fermentation or anaerobic cellular respiration rather than oxygenation.) This is why clean air and adequate oxygen consumption, facilitated by active exercise, are vital to a healthy human body.

Besides DHEA's ability to block glucocorticoid destruction of normal cellular metabolism, studies have shown that there appears to be a connection between the body's deficient DHEA levels and the onset of *some* types of cancer. These include kidney, bladder, liver and gastric cancers.

DHEA has been shown to inhibit tumor development by blocking critical metabolic links associated with cancer tumor growth. The most documented and highly regarded link has been DHEA's ability to block G6PD (glucose-6-phosphate dehydrogenase), an enzyme found in the liver and the kidneys that supplies sugar via the pentose shunt (the process of metabolic breakdown of five-carbon sugars) which otherwise stimulates abnormal cell proliferation associated with cancerous tumors. (Ennas et. al., 1987, Feo et. al., 1990 and Kalimi et. al., 1990). For decades it has been well documented that high levels of G6PD are found in many carcinomas.

In other studies conducted on tumors, DHEA was shown to inhibit protein synthesis (Schultz, 1991) and specific enzyme production associated with cancer development within tumors (Merriman et. al., 1982). This demonstrated role of DHEA in inhibiting tumor growth is exciting news to cancer researchers. It can be inferred from these studies that the monitoring and correcting of deficient DHEA and DHEAS levels in cancer patients might be a helpful tool in arresting some types of cancer. However, raising circulating DHEA levels could spell trouble with one type of cancer.

BREAST CANCER

As already mentioned earlier, there was a long-term study of the citizens of the island of Guernsey in Great Britain. The island's population has been under constant medical observation for decades, similar to the Farmington, N.Y., study here in the U.S. The island provided researchers with a living laboratory. Of 5,000 women between the ages of 30 and 59, those who had maintained serum levels of less than 10% of the expected DHEA concentrations for a period of 10 years or more all developed and eventually died of breast cancer (Bulbrook et. al., 1971). Theories based on these findings were tested in experiments with tissue culture cells. Dr. Schwartz placed cells showing the breakage of chromosomes that lead to cancer in a medium containing DHEA. There was no breakage of the chromosomes and no transformation of these cells into cancer. However, there were a number of subsequent studies with findings that were not so positive about DHEA and its relationship to breast cancer in post-menopausal women (Barrett-Conner 1990, Poortman et. al., 1975 and Seymour-Munn et. al., 1982).

Two hormonal factors are involved in breast cancer— androgen deficiency and estradiol excess. Results have shown an association between breast cancer and DHEA; *low* DHEA concentrations in premenopausal women is linked to breast cancer, but it is with *high* DHEA concentrations that it is linked in postmenopausal women. It is suggested that in pre-menopausal women, low DHEA stimulates tumor cell growth by leaving estradiol uninhibited, because DHEA is not manu-facturing androgens to oppose it. This apparently increases the risk of breast cancer. Estrogen is considered a cancer initiator. In the postmenopausal woman, high DHEA levels cause the body to produce estradiol because of the reduced circulating levels of estrogen brought about by the shut down of the ovaries. In a postmenopausal woman's body, as a response to the decreased production of her own estrogen, an abundance of DHEA, caused by its supplementation or her naturally occurring high levels, will be pushed into the estradiol production pathway and thereby stimulate tumor cell growth. This is important information concerning hormone-dependent cancers, like uterine and breast cancers (Ebeling et. al., 1994). The implications are that correcting decreased

DHEA levels by supplying DHEA as a supplement may be warranted in a premenopausal woman. However, for a postmenopausal woman, increasing DHEA levels above the natural declining levels could promote some of these hormone-dependent cancers.

POLYCYSTIC OVARIES

Although polycystic ovaries are not linked to cancer, there is evidence that women prone to the occurrence of the cystic condition of their ovaries have high DHEAS levels, especially in women with fat accumulation across the abdomen rather than the hips and thighs (Douchi et. al., 1995).

PROSTATE CANCER

With DHEA's androgenic ability, the question is whether DHEA supplementation raises testosterone levels in men. In a study conducted in 1990 with extremely high doses of DHEA supplements (1,200 mg. per day), dihydrotestosterone (DHT) levels were found to have doubled (Roberts and Fitten, 1990). Very high DHEA dosage causing this high level of DHT means serious consequences for many men. As a man ages, his internal hormone levels alter with the naturally declining testosterone hormone being converting into the more active DHT. This form of testosterone, DHT, has been implicated in the growth of tissues associated with enlargement of the prostate. This enlargement termed *benign prostatic hypertrophy* (BPH) is considered normal by most physicians. 50% of all men by the age of 60 and 80% of all men past the age of 70 suffer with the condition. Roughly 20% of swollen prostate

Hormone Changes with DHEA Supplementation

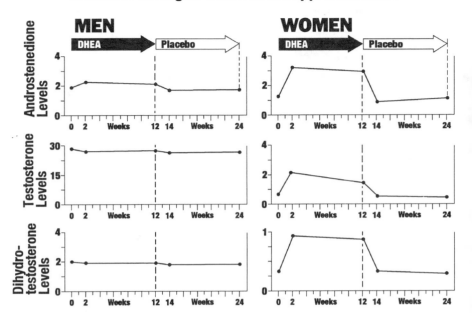

After six months of treatment with 50 mg. of DHEA daily, Morales and colleagues found no change in serum testosterone or dihydrotestosterone in men. The same dosage however, caused a significant increase in androstenedione, testosterone and dihydrotestosterone in women.

cases are the result of cancer. Prostate cancer is the most common cancer among men with 165,000 cases reported annually. It ranks second only to lung cancer as a leading cause of cancer deaths among men. Based on the results of this study, it would appear that DHEA at this *high* dosage level could be cancer provoking.

A subsequent study conducted in 1994 utilized a greatly reduced dose of 50 mg. per day which did not adversely affect testosterone or dihydrotestosterone levels in men

(Morales, 1994). This dosage is adequate to restore DHEA to the youthful, not dangerous, levels and is what many physicians prescribe. It could provide DHEA's anti-cancer rather than a cancer-provoking effect on prostates.

However, this 50 mg. per day dosage did significantly alter women's testosterone and dihydrotestosterone levels, raising them dramatically. DHEA's disturbance of the balance of sex hormones and its potential increase in the risk of heart disease are complications that must be carefully considered before its supplementation can be recommended to postmenopausal women.

DIETARY CONSIDERATIONS

A vegetarian diet appears to deplete DHEA, according to Drs. Kalimi and Regelson in their important book *The Biologic Role of Dehydroepiandrosterone (DHEA)*. The finding is not unrealistic when one considers that DHEA synthesis is dependent on LDL (low-density lipoprotein) cholesterol, a substance not associated with strict vegetarian diets.

There have been claims that plant sterols called phytosterols, most notably stigmasterol, beta sitosterol and campesterol, can meet the needs of strict vegetarians in regards to their steroid production. These plant sterols are found in a variety of plants, most notably yams. However, the naturally occurring levels in plants are significantly low and require a tremendous intake of plant foods.

Unfortunately, many individuals who practice vegetarianism in this country do not manage their diets well. Many restrict themselves to pastas and dairy products rather than including beans, legumes, and a *wide* variety of vegetables and grains.

In well-managed vegetarian diets, the need for sterols is generally met.

Unlike the diets of most other cultures that have traditional dietary customs fine tuned to specific environmental and physical needs, the Standard American Diet (SAD) with its high fat and high carbohydrate content is sadly deficient. In today's world, food has to be fast and easy to prepare. Many individual and family schedules demand it. Few have the time or the energy to devote quality time to food preparation. A good, well-balanced diet requires a full kitchen, not just a microwave.

Vegetarianism aside, there is another popular dietary sacred cow of the uninformed trying to be more health conscious which can negatively affect the body's ability to produce DHEA —the "eliminate fat" craze that has swept the nation.

In some instances, the need to reduce fat has gone too far. The good cholesterol/ bad cholesterol concept has been oversimplified for the public. There is a valid place in human physiology for LDL cholesterol. Granted, most Americans **who are also sedentary** have a seriously high level of fat accounting for their daily caloric intake. Some surveys put the figure as high as 45-50%. Remarkably, for some genetic groups, relatively high fat intake is about right. For example, certain Native Americans are physiologically well fit for high protein and high fat diets but unfit for high carbohydrate diets. The serious dietary mistake most native peoples are making is high intake of carbohydrates (breads, pastas, rice, sugar and potatoes) that only recently have been added to their diets. This is a classic example of genetic genocide being perpetrated by the narrow overview of "dietary guidelines for the normal individual." Normal is relative.

This increase of carbohydrates introduced to an age-old essentially meat-eating people who were accustomed to consuming low to marginal intakes of starch (camas root and pinon nuts) is devastating to certain Native Americans and is contributing to their high rates of insipid diabetes, obesity and heart disease (all linked in clinical studies to low DHEA levels). The consumption of alcohol, a simple carbohydrate, is particularly detrimental.

For many of northern and eastern European descent, a level of protein/fat at 25-30% of total intake is near optimal. Higher cholesterol levels were necessary for some groups, most notably central and eastern Europeans, for survival against the bitter winter cold. Because of this adaptation of storing fat to protect the body from cold, these groups have higher "set points" for circulating cholesterol. If diet does not provide enough LDL cholesterol, the liver will produce it in order to meet genetic requirements. For this genetic group, total cholesterol levels of up to 240 are actually normal and efforts to lower them will be met with little success, despite cholesterol-lowering drugs and dietary restrictions.

Among black Americans, there is the possibility of wide ranges of optimal fat intakes considering the diversity in diets native to the African continent as a whole. For example, the diet of the *Masai* of East Africa with its extremely high protein and fat content consisting primarily of milk mixed with blood and meat is to be distinguished from the diet of a West African, with his high consumption of peanuts, yams and cereal grains. This wide diversity occurs in Asian diets as well.

The nutritional content of some foods cannot necessarily

be assimilated as efficiently by some racial groups or certain individuals. The true impediment to a Standard American Diet is the "melting pot" phenomenon. In my own genetic background, for example, I am of northern European, coastal European and Native American descent. From their father's side, my children are also of eastern European extraction (Ukrainian and Khazitstan). These varied bloodline combinations and others just as complicated are the norm in this country and represent radical differences in genetically influenced physiologies with radically different dietary needs between individuals vital to keeping their bodies functioning well.

One basic need of the body is the inclusion of mono-saturated LDL cholesterol in the diet. Ignoring a body's inherent need for *some* cholesterol and fat sets up a whole range of progressive degenerative problems. A low-cholesterol, low-fat diet taken *too far* is dangerous, most notably affecting the adrenal production of steroid hormones necessary for growth and reproduction. Without a readily available source of sterols, the adrenals' ability to produce the sex hormones, corticoids and DHEA is impaired.

An essential premise is that with diet, as with all things, moderation is the key. Understanding an individual's particular nutritional requirements is complicated. Assessing biochemical individuality associated with genetic predispositions is central to good health. **No single program, diet or supplement is good for _all_ individuals or in _all_ circumstances**. Because individually there are so many variables to be considered including different genetics, environments and stress levels, common sense and education are the best tools for determining what is best for you.

TO YAM OR NOT TO YAM

Popular "DHEA precursor" products based on *Dioscorea villosa* (wild yam) or *Dioscorea mexicana* (Mexican yam) claim DHEA activity. These claims demand closer scrutiny.

Herbalists, as well as pharmacists, list the active steroidal ingredient of *Dioscorea* as a steroid saponin called diosgenin. The body metabolizes diosgenin into pregnenolone. Pregnenolone can then take one of two routes in the body. Based on physiological needs, pregnenolone will either break down directly into progesterone *or*, in a two-step process, into DHEA. The advertisers of the "DHEA precusor" products are ignoring this very interesting progesterone pathway in order to capitalize on the increasing public interest in DHEA. Pregnenolone in its own right confers dramatic benefits and should be acknowledged for its progesterone pathway over its DHEA potential.

Dioscorea is a commonly used substance in the Chinese pharmacopoeia. It is specifically related to deficient *kidney yin* and is a component in *empty blood tonics*. Its use in tonics come from formulas that are thousands of years old. DHEA could be the modern equivalent of these kidney yin tonics. In the West, Dioscorea villosa has been used as the principal source of manufactured steroids since steroid precursors in it were first discovered in 1936. Steroid drugs derived from diosgenin include corticosteroids, oral contraceptives, androgens and estrogens. **Dioscorea does not contain the actual hormones nor DHEA. Any product containing only Mexican or wild yam that claims to have DHEA in it is mislabeled.** The body must provide the enzymes to produce the processes needed for the production of those hormones from dioscorea. Because of the natural decline in DHEA and, by inference, the body's consequent reduction in the enzymatic activities associated with it, metabolization of DHEA from pregnelonone would also be reduced. Instead, after age 30, pregnenolone would more readily follow the progesterone production route. Through this route, the progesterone goes on to produce corticoid steroids as well as estrogens and androgens, but not DHEA.

Progesterone in and of itself offers very significant benefits. Many of those benefits are remarkably similar to those associated with DHEA. John R. Lee, M.D., conducted important research on progesterone and provides the following list of benefits associated with the steroid:

- helps burn fat for energy
- acts as antidepressant
- acts as natural diuretic
- facilitates thyroid hormone action
- normalizes blood sugar levels

- restores libido
- restores proper cell oxygen levels
- deters fibrocystic breast condition
- reduces risk of endometrial cancer
- helps prevent breast cancer
- stimulates bone building
- acts as precursor of corticosterone production

In short, progesterone deficiency (which pregnenolone can correct) leads to many of the symptoms associated with PMS, depression and fibrocystic conditions which are related to unopposed estrogen. According to Dr. Lee, many women's progesterone levels fall to zero as early as the perimenopausal stage, approximately 10 years before the onset of actual menopause.

Androgen production stimulated by DHEA in postmenopausal women has been shown to be of some value in relieving a host of psychosomatic symptoms including irritability, nervousness, forgetfulness, crying spells, excitability and insomnia. DHEA as a neurosteroid is synthesized naturally from pregnenolone in the brain. Pregnenolone *in the brain* is more likely to produce DHEA, even though in the endocrine system it is more likely to produce progesterone. Testosterone is currently being prescribed to alleviate these symptoms, but its supplementation can increase the risk of CVD in these women. Pregnenolone should be recommended instead, because it may be less apt to increase this risk.

Pregnenolone was widely used in the 1940's in this country as an anti-inflammatory in the treatment of arthritis. Use of this natural product dramatically declined when a pharmaceutical company was able to isolate cortisone and patent and manufacture it as hydrocortisone or prednisone. However, based on the destructive capabilities of cortisone treatments unbuffered by the synergistic steroids (including DHEA) that occur naturally in pregnenolone breakdown, using pregnenolone as an anti-inflammatory to treat arthritis and fibromyalgia should be investigated before resorting to prednisone.

Because of pregnenolone's more diverse abilities, it should be recommended for women who are over the age of 50. Except in cases of obvious declines in DHEA levels associated with disease conditions determined by blood tests, pregnenolone would be a more comprehensive choice over DHEA supplements for postmenopausal women.

TAKING DHEA AS A SUPPLEMENT

All the critical questions about supplementation, how much to take, when to take it, what kind to take, have been the subject of some controversy. The dosages given in some of the clinical trials (up to 2,400 mg./day) have been extreme and should be taken *only* when under close medical supervision and *only* in cases such as AIDS or some other serious auto-immune disease.

There is considerable concern about creating an adrenal dependency for supplemental DHEA because of the very destructive way that synthetic cortisone treatments affect the adrenal output of natural cortisol. The regulating system (the negative feed back system) pertinent to cortisone therapy problems is apparently not relevant to DHEA output. Currently, there appears to be no threat of DHEA dependency.

Most practitioners feel that a blood baseline level of DHEA and DHEAS should first be established before prescribing the substance. Under no circumstances should DHEA be given to a young person unless a particular health condition warrants testing for the DHEA/DHEAS levels, as in the case with AIDS. Otherwise, supplementation is generally inadvisable until age 35. For the aging population, the time of day the blood test is taken to determine DHEA/DHEAS levels is critical to interpreting the lab results. DHEA levels are at their highest diurnal levels in the morning and fall off significantly during the day.

Because of natural diurnal rhythms, DHEA supplements usually should be taken immediately upon rising in the morning.

Supplementing DHEA would not be entirely safe for postmenopausal women, except in cases of systemic lupus erythematosus (SLE) and under close supervision. For women in this group, pregnenolone would be a safer and more comprehensive choice. Pregnenolone requires much lower doses— 5 mg. to a maximum dose of 100 mg.

Because of the inherent increase in androgens associated with DHEA supplementation in women, it might and might not prove beneficial. The androgen testosterone is linked to female libido. DHEA's ability to increase androgen production and thereby potentially increase sex drive could be a rather nice side effect from its supplementation. Regarding the bad side effect of unwanted facial hair (hirsutism)—with its appearance, supplementation should be halted immediately until the symptom subsides. If supplementation is resumed, it should be in much lower doses. In perimenopausal women between the ages of 45-50, a dose between 25-50 mg. per day of DHEA would be appropriate.

For men, 50-100 mg. of DHEA appears to be beneficial for cancer prevention, as well as reducing their risk of cardiovascular disease.

There are a number of forms of DHEA that are sold through compounding labs or through some health food stores and via mail order (see Resources Section). Generally, the DHEA of lab origin is bound with an oil which makes it more stable for passing through the gut and into the bloodstream. Most advocates feel the liquid sublingual version (absorbed under the tongue) is superior in that the DHEA passes through the sublingual membrane directly into the bloodstream, bypassing the gut altogether.

More extensive studies and long-term research is needed. The range of dosages utilized in the studies has been from a moderate 50 mg. a day to the excessively high levels of 2,400 mg. daily. **No one knows what are the long-term effects of taking doses exceeding the normal output of healthy young adrenals. The average recommended dose should not exceed 100 mg. per day for men and 50 mg. for women, allowing for varying absorbtion levels. Better to err on the side of caution until more studies can be done.**

The probability of extensive studies being conducted is not great. The FDA pulled all DHEA off the health food market in 1985 because the product under then-existing models of endocrine biochemistry showed it to be a precursor to steroid anabolic hormones (regulated by the FDA) with the possibility of abuse. Subsequent studies have suggested that the types and amounts of steroids DHEA supplements produce do not lead to excessive production of the steroids that are commonly abused.

Due to interpretations of the recently implemented *Dietary Supplement, Health and Education Act*, DHEA and pregnenolone have once again become available in the health food market. Based on the fact that these are naturally occurring substances and are derived from substances that are fundamental to human physiology, cholesterol, DHEA and pregnenolone are now considered nutritional supplements. One of the concerns of the FDA regarding the availability of DHEA within the health food industry is the claim of "DHEA activity" made by the companies who are marketing the products. Another concern is that the health food industry has no regulations concerning the quality of a product; the quality of non-prescription DHEA and pregnenolone would be entirely self-regulated by the individual manufacturers. Consumers have to depend on the integrity of these manufacturers in making their purchases. Few consumers have the ability to run independent tests on a product, so that a degree of risk of adulteration and fraud is of course present with non-prescription products.

There is a great deal of concern within the medical community and with alternative practitioners regarding the unknown potentials of supplementing DHEA, pregnenolone and another hormone now available to the general public, melatonin, because of the admittedly vast numbers of unknown factors concerning the endocrine system. There is a great deal *more* about this intricate system that is still a mystery. The emphasis of a moderate approach to DHEA, pregnenolone and melatonin supplementation coupled with continuing research and self-education is necessary if you are attempting therapy without professional supervision.

Only pharmaceutical companies have the funds available to support long-term studies to bring a product to market.

Mistakes were made regarding DHEA-compound registration by researchers after the initial studies were conducted. Dr. Schwartz published his work concerning the anti-cancer effect of DHEA in 1975 and, because he failed to apply for a certain type of patent within the year of its introduction, no company can now hold exclusive or full rights to that compound. This error has successfully discouraged any company from spending the money needed to further study DHEA and its effects.

Federal funds for such projects are virtually non-existent. A quagmire of regulatory rules, medical/business ethics and politics will continue to hinder the process of making extensive DHEA research possible.

GLOSSARY

adrenal—the endocrine gland which sits on top of both respective kidneys.

ACTH (Adrenocorticotropin Hormone)—the pituitary hormone responsible for stimulating the adrenal cortex to release hormones which are essential to growth, development and the continued functioning of the adrenal cortex.

aflatoxin—a toxin produced by strains of the *Aspergillus fungus* that has carcinogenic effects on experimental animals. Aflatoxins are commonly found within the food chain, especially in peanuts, feed corn and dairy products.

anabolic—the constructive phase of metabolism. It is the ability to take from the blood substances required for repair and growth, converting non-living material into cellular cytoplasm.

analogue—a compound that is structurally similar to another.

androgen—a substance that stimulates the development of male characteristics as in testosterone and androsterone. In the female, 90% of these androgens are produced in the adrenal; in the male 60-70% are adrenally produced.

angiotensin—a substance that causes the contraction of the capillaries and arteries thus raising blood pressure. It is formed by the interaction of renin from the kidneys and a serum protein.

anti-inflammatory—a substance that counteracts inflammation. Inflammation is generally indicated by heat and swelling.

autonomic nervous system—the part of the nervous system that is responsible for the involuntary functions of the body such as breathing, digestion and endocrine function.

BPH (Benign Prostate Hypertrophy)—a non-malignant swelling of the prostate gland.

biosynthetic pathway—metabolic pathway in which the body converts sugar into fatty acids for future use.

bone apatates—the foundation of bone structures composed of calcium, magnesium and phosphorus compounds.

cancer initiator—a substance that initiates abnormal cell replication leading to cancer (also known as an inductor).

cancer promoter—a condition or substance that promotes the proliferation of cancer.

carcinogenic—a toxin or condition that stimulates the production of cancer cells.

catabolic—the destructive phase of metabolism. This phase involves the tearing down of existing structures to smaller units for repair or energy.

catecholamines—derived from the amino acid tyrosine, they have a marked effect on the nervous system involved in the "fight or flight" and para-sympathetic responses to danger and stress.

CD-4—thymus-produced immune factors also called T-helper cells.

CD-8—thymus-produced immune factors also called T-suppressor cells.

CFIDS (Chronic Fatigue Immune Deficiency Syndrome)—a disorder of the immune system displaying symptoms of fatigue and general malaise.

chi—a Chinese word that is best expressed as body energy and vitality.

cholesterol—a chemical structure that is responsible for providing the foundation molecule of steroid hormones such as sex hormones and adrenal corticoids.

circadian cycle—natural body rhythms that are set up by the pineal gland from exposure to light, influenced by seasonal changes as well as daily rhythms of the sun and moon.

DHT (Dihydrotestosterone)—a breakdown product of testosterone that is implicated in prostate cancer.

diosgenin—a steroid saponin found in plants, particularly yams, that can produce pregnenolone in the human body and which potentially can be converted into DHEA.

diurnal rhythm—daily cycles, especially involving functions that occur during daylight hours rather than at night.

endocrine system—a body system that includes 12 ductless glands and a number of tissue sites which excrete hormones or hormone precursors.

epinephrine—more commonly referred to as adrenaline. A product of the medulla portion of the adrenal that stimulates the so-called "fight or flight" response.

estrogen—from the Greek, meaning "a mad desire to reproduce." The term estrogen is generally applied to any substance that produces secondary female characteristics as well as the cyclical changes in the vaginal and uterine endothelial tissues. The body utilizes estrogen in the forms of estradiol, esterone and estriol.

fatty acid—major building blocks of fat in the human body. Linoleic, linolenic and oleic acids are essential fatty acids. Fats are generally classified as saturated (carbons linked together by single bonds) and unsaturated (carbons linked by one or more double or triple bonds).

fibromyalgia—a condition of unknown origin characterized by fatigue and pain, particularly at trigger points generally specific to the muscle groups of the shoulder and neck regions.

GAS (General Adaptation Syndrome)—a theory developed by Dr. Hans Selye regarding the effect of long-term stress on the endocrine system and the endocrine's subsequent impact on the body.

glucocorticoids—a general classification of adrenal cortex hormones that are primarily responsible for protecting the body against stress. The prefix gluco- denotes the fact that the hormone is attached to a glucose (sugar) molecule. High levels can be detrimental.

glycogen—a form of glucose stored for future use.

G6PD (Glucose 6 Phosphate Dehydrogenase)—an enzyme that is important in converting glycerol to glucose. Involved in the energy-producing pathway to convert stored sugars into readily usable glucose and in the biosynthetic pathway which converts glucose into fatty acids for storage.

hemopoiesis—the formation of blood cells.

hirsutism—excessive hair growth in areas usually not hairy.

hormone—a substance secreted by a gland or organ that stimulates another part of the body.

HRT (Hormone Replacement Therapy)—a therapy prescribed for the hormonal treatment of menopausal symptoms brought on by age or removal of the ovaries.

hypothalamus—buried deep within the brain, it gets information from the forebrain that has been interpreted by the amygdala and the thalamus. Based on its interpretation of stimuli, the hypothalamus will stimulate the pituitary.

IGF-1 (Insulin-like Growth Factor-1)—a growth hormone that is produced in the liver and other tissue sites to stimulate immune function.

IL-2 (Interleukin-2)—a cytokine specific to the ability of the body to stimulate proper T-cell functions.

kidney jing—In traditional Chinese medicine, it is essential kidney energy that is associated with reproductive ability and good health.

kidney yang—a form of kidney energy that is responsible for the containment of the kidney *yin* in TCM.

kidney yin—the "essence of vitality" stored in the kidney as understood in TCM. It supplies energy to all other tissues in the body and aids food digestion.

meridians—channels or pathways through which *chi* or energy passes. In TCM, there are 12 main meridians based on organ pairings.

mineralocorticoid—a corticoid produced by the adrenal cortex responsible for the maintenance of sodium and potassium levels.

mutagenic—that which causes a mutation in the DNA of a cell.

otitis media—middle ear infection that especially afflicts children.

pineal—an endocrine gland situated near the pituitary deep within the brain that interprets light. From this information, the body establishes circadian and diurnal rhythms.

pituitary—an endocrine gland situated between the two lobes of the brain producing stimulating hormones that orchestrate basic bodily functions.

precursor hormone—a hormone that provides the structure for a subsequent hormone. DHEA is a precursor hormone for progesterone, estrogens and testosterones.

pregnenolone—a precursor hormone that can be converted into either progesterone or, possibly, DHEA within the body.

progesterone—a sex hormone produced by women, the supplementation of which improves bone density for the prevention of osteoporosis.

prostate—a partly muscular, partly glandular body that is situated at the base of the male urethra.

release factors—chemicals produced in the hypothalamus which stimulate the anterior pituitary to produce hormones that further stimulate glands and tissue sites. For example, FSHRF (follicle-stimulating hormone release factor) is responsible for stimulating the production of an egg from the ovary.

SLE (Systemic Lupus Erythematosus) –an autoimmune disease primarily afflicting women which attacks collagen and the kidneys.

steroid hormones—sex hormone and hormones of the adrenal cortex that have as their foundation molecule sterol, a product of cholesterol.

testosterone—a steroid hormone responsible for masculinizing characteristics. Testosterone is *usually* classed as an androgen in the female body.

vasoconstrictor—a substance that causes the reduction of the diameter of capillaries and arteries of the blood system.

RESOURCES

DHEA by prescription is considerably cheaper in cost than it is through mail-order suppliers. DHEA and pregnenolone are obtained generally through "compounding labs" and often cannot be purchased at most local drug stores even with a prescription. Following is a list of compounding labs and mail-order sources of DHEA and pregnenolone:

With a prescription

Women's International Pharmacy
5708 Monona Dr.
Madison, WI 53716
    or
13925 Meeker Blvd.
Suite #13
Sun City West, AZ 85375
1-800-279-5708

College Pharmacy
833 N. Tejon St.
Colorado Springs, CO 80903
1-800-888-9358

No prescription necessary

Life Enhancement Products, Inc.
PO Box 751390
Petaluma, CA 94975
1-800-543-3873

Peggy's Health Center
151 First St.
Los Altos, CA 94022
1-800-862-9191 (or locally)
1-415-948-9191

Home Link Pharmacy
2650 Elm Ave. #104
Long Beach, CA 90806
1-800-272-4767

ABOUT THE AUTHOR

 **Alana Pascal** is a certified Clinical Nutritionist who has been in the alternative health field for 25 years. Because of her comprehensive knowledge of Eastern and Western medicine, anthropology and biochemistry, she has helped define a new niche in medicine as a *holistic practitioner.* She now lives in the Pacific Northwest.

Teaching and writing have become her focus in order that others will understand, as we enter the 21st century, how we should be changing our approach to health and disease. Her thoroughly researched, writing and easy-to-understand style make her books especially informative about otherwise-complicated scientific subjects.

Her first book, *Kombucha...How-To And What It's All About* first published in 1995, was critically acclaimed for its research and wealth of information in sorting out the myths and controversies surrounding the new "mushroom" tea health craze. Less than one year after its first publication, it became a Book-of-the-Month Club selection.

BIBLIOGRAPHY

JOURNALS

Barrett-Conner E; Friedlander NJ; Khaw KT. Dehydroepiandrosterone sulfate and breast cancer risk. Cancer Research, 1990 October, 50 (20) : 6571-6574.

Barret-Conner E; Knaw KT; Yen SSC. A prospective study of dehydroepiandrosterone sulfate, mortality and cardiovascular disease. New England Journal of Medicine, 1986, 315 : 1519-1524.

Birkenhager-Gillesse EG; Derkson J; Lagaay AM. Dehydroepiandrosterone sulphate (DHEAS) in the oldest old, ages 85 and over. Annals of the New York Academy of Sciences, 1994 May 31, 719 : 543-552.

Brignardello E; Cassoni P; Migliardi M; Pizzini A; Di Monaco M; Boccuzzi G; Massobrio M. Dehydroepiandrosterone concentration in breast cancer tissue is related to its plasma gradient across the mammary gland. Breast Cancer Research and Treatment, 1995, 33 (2) : 171-177.

Daynes RA; Araneo BA. Contrasting effects of glucocorticoids on the capacity of T-cells to produce the growth factor interleukin-2 and interleukin-4. Eur. J Immunol, 1990, 19 : 2319-2325.

de Peretti E; Forest M. Pattern of plasma dehydroepiandrosterone sulfate levels in humans from birth to adulthood. Evidence for testicular production. Journal of Clinical Endocrinology and Metabolism 1978, 47 (3) : 572-577.

Douchi T; Ijuin H; Nakamura S; Oki T; Yamamoto S; Nagata Y. Body fat distribution in women with polycystic ovary syndrome. Obstetrics and Gynecology, 1995 October, 86 (4 Pt 1) : 516-519.

Dyner TS; Lang W; Geaga J; Golub A; Stites D; Winger E; Galamarini M; Masterson J; Jacobson MA. An open-label dose-escalation trial of oral dehydroepiandrosterone tolerance and pharmacokinetics in patients with HIV disease. Journal of Acquired Immune Deficiency Syndrome. 1993 May, 6 (5) : 459-465.

Ebeling P; Koivisto VA. Physiological importance of dehydroepiandrosterone. Lancet, 1994 June 11, 343 (8911) : 1479-1481.

Glaser JL; Brind JL; Vogelman JH; Eisner MJ; Dillbeck MC; Willace RK; Chopra D; Orentreich N. Elevated serum dehydroepiandrosterone sulfate levels in practitioners of Transcendental Mediation (TM) and TM-Sidhi programs. Journal of Behavioral Medicine, 1992 August, 15 (4) : 327-341.

Holsboer F; Grasser A; Freiss E; Wiedemann K. Steroid Effects on central neurons and implications for psychiatric and neurological disorders. Annals of the New York of Sciences, 1994 November 30, 746 : 345-359.

LaCroix AZ; Yano K; Reed DM. Dehydroepiandrosterone sulfate, incidence of myocardial infarction, and extent of atherosclerosis in men. Circulation, 1992 November, 86 (5) : 1529-1535.

Loria RM; Padgett DA. Androstenediol regulates systemic resistance against lethal infections in mice. Archives of Virology, 1992, 127 (1-4) : 103-115.

Morales AJ; Nolan JJ; Nelson JC; Yen SS. Effects of replacement dose of dehydroepiandrosterone in men and women of advancing age. Journal of Endocrinology and Metabolism, 1994 June, 78 (6) : 1360-1367.

Mulder JW; Frissen PH; Krijnen P; Endert E; deWolf F; Goudmnit J; Masterson JG; Lang JM. Dehydroepiandrosterone as predictor for progression to AIDS in asymptomatic human immunodeficiency virus-infected men. Journal of Infectious Diseases, 1992 March, 165 (3) : 413-418.

Nestler JE; Clore JN; Blackard WG. Dehydroepiandrosterone: the "missing link" between hyperinsulinemia and atherosclerosis. Faseb Journal, 1992 September 6 (12) : 3073-3075.

Nottlemann E; Susman E; Inoff-Germain G; Cutler G; Loriaus D; Chrousos G. Developmental processes in early adolescence. Relationships between adolescent adjustment problems and chronologic age, pubertal stage, and puberty-related serum hormone levels. Journal of Pediatrics, 1987 March, 473-480.

Rasmussen KR; Healey MC; Cheng L; Yang S. Effects of dehydroepiandrosterone in immunosuppressed adult mice infected with Cryptosporidium parvum. Journal of Parasitology, 1995 June, 81 (3) : 429-433.

Regelson W; Kalimi M. Dehydroepiandrosterone (DHEA)—the multifunctional steroid. Effects on the CNS, cell proliferation, metabolic and vascular, clinical and other effects. Mechanism of action? Annals of the New York Academy of Sciences, 1994 May 31, 719 : 553-563.

Regelson W; Loria R; Kalimi M. Dehydroepiandrosterone (DHEA)—the "Mother Steroid" 1. Immunologic Action. Annals of the New York Academy of Sciences, 1994 May 31, 719 : 553-564.

Sambrook PN et al. Sex hormone status and osteoporosis in postmenopausal women with rheumatoid arthritis. Arthritis Rheum., 1988, 31 : 973-978.

Slowinska-Srzednicka J; Malczewska B; Srzednicki M; Chotkowska L; Brezezinska A; Zgliczynski W; Ossowski M; Jeske W; Zgliczynski S; Sadowski Z. Hyperinsulinaemia and decreased plasma levels of dehydroepiandrosterone sulfate in premenopausal women with coronary heart disease. Journal of Internal Medicine, 1995 May, 237 (5) : 465-472.

Suzuki T; Suzuki N; Engleman EG; Mizushima Y; Sakane T. Low serum levels of dehydroepiandrosterone may cause deficient IL-2 production by lymphocytes in patients with systemic lupus erythematosus (SLE). Clinical and Experimental Immunology, 1995, 99 (2) : 251-255.

Touitou Y. Effects of aging on endocrine and neuroendocrine rhythms in humans. Hormone Research, 1995, 43 (1-3) : 12-19.

Vatz RE; Weinberg LE. Overreacting to attention deficit disorder. USA Today 1995, January v123 : 84.

von Vollenhoven RF; Engleman EG; McGuire JL. An open study of dehydroepiandrosterone in systemic lupus erythematosus. Arthritis and Rheumatism, 1994 September, 37 (9) : 1305-1310.

BOOKS

Beijing College et. al. *Essentials of Chinese Acupuncture.* Foreign Language Press, Beijing, China, 1980.

Burton Goldberg Group. *Alternative Medicine.* Future Medicine Publishing, Inc., Fife, WA, 1994.

Dean, W.: Morgenthaler, J. *Smart Drugs and Nutrients.* Health Freedom Publications, Menlo Park, CA, 1991.

Goleman, D. *Emotional Intelligence.* Bantum, New York, NY,1995.

Wilson et. al. *Harrison's Principles of Internal Medicine.* McGraw-Hill, New York, NY, 1991.

Kahn, C. *Beyond the Helix-DNA and the Quest for Longevity.* Times Books, New York, NY,1985.

Kalimi, M.: Regelson, W. (Eds.) *The Biological Role of Dehydroepiandrosterone (DHEA).* Walter de Gruyter, New York, NY, 1990.

Kaptchuk, T. *The Web That Has No Weaver.* Congdon and Weed, Chicago, IL,1983.

Lebowitz, M. *Body Mechanics.* MMI Press, Harrisville, NH, 1984.

Mills, S. *The Essential Book of Herbal Medicine.* Arkana, New York, NY, 1991.

Moore, N. *Bountiful Health, Boundless Energy, Brilliant Youth (The Facts About DHEA).* Charis Publishing Co., Dallas, TX, 1994.

Mowrey, DB. *The Scientific Validation of Herbal Medicine.* Cormorant Books, 1986.

Rosenbaum, M.: Susser, M. *Solving the Puzzle of Chronic Fatigue Syndrome.* Life Sciences Press, Tacoma, WA, 1992.

Selye, H. *The Stress of Life.* McGraw-Hill, New York, NY, 1978.

INDEX

ORDER FORM

BOOKS BY ALANA PASCAL

KOMBUCHA...How-To And What It's All About $12.95
128 pages including illustrations, glossary and index
ISBN # 0-9645352-0-3

Kombucha, also known as "mushroom tea," is considered a miracle source of healing and energy. Thousands are drinking and brewing the tea. It reportedly detoxifies the liver, reduces grey hair and wrinkles, increases energy, balances the pH system and much more. In this critically acclaimed book, you will find a wealth of information surrounding this mysterious yeast and bacteria culture.

DHEA...The Fountain of Youth Discovered? $12.95
128 pages including illustrations, glossary and index
ISBN #0-9645352-1-1

DHEA *(dehydroepiandrosterone)* is an adrenal hormone naturally produced in large quantities during our youth. Its production decreases around the age of 30 and current research has found this hormone could be part of the link between youth and aging. This book is written for both the consumer and health practitioner so that informed decisions can be made regarding its use.

Please add 8.25% for books shipped to California addresses.(Do not include shipping amount when calculating sales tax.) All books are sent first class mail. Add $3.00 for shipping and handling in the United States and Canada. Outside the U.S. and Canada, send $7.00 for shipping and handling. Add $1.50 for each additional book to be sent to any one U.S. address. Send Check or Money order. No credit cards accepted.

Quantity		Title
_____	$12.95 each	*Kombucha...How-To And What It's All About*
_____	$12.95 each	*DHEA...The Fountain of Youth Discovered?*

PLEASE SEND THE BOOK(S) TO:

Name _____

Address _____

City & State _____ Zip _____

The Van der Kar Press
PO Box 189
Malibu, CA 90265-0189